Stadium Stories:

# San Francisco 49ers

Stadium Stories™ Series

Stadium Stories:

# San Francisco 49ers

Dennis Georgatos

INSIDERS' GUIDE®

GUILFORD, CONNECTICUT
AN IMPRINT OF THE GLOBE PEQUOT PRESS

**INSIDERS' GUIDE**®

Text design: Casey Shain

Cover photos: *front cover:* Joe Montana (Joe Robbins); *back cover:* top,
Frankie Albert (AP); bottom, Bill Walsh (Ed Reinke/AP)

Library of Congress Cataloging-in-Publication Data is available.

ISBN 0-7627-3792-1

Manufactured in the United States of America
First Edition/First Printing

This book is for the players whose labor, sweat, and sacrifice brought a great game life, not to mention giving me and many others something to write about. And this is for Gregory, Daniel, and Barbara Georgatos.

# Contents

# Acknowledgments

**Many good people** helped me during the course of writing this book. Among them are R. C. Owens, Gary Plummer, Jim Saccomano, 49ers historian Donn Sinn, pro football librarian Joe Cronin, Bill Walsh, Jane Walsh, John Madden, and Nancy Schafer. Thanks for taking my phone calls, answering my questions, and just giving me the time of day. Many thanks to my colleagues Greg Beacham, Rick Eymer, Kevin Lynch, Phil Barber, and Matt Maiocco; to editors Jim Gigliotti, Mary Norris, and Mike and Ellen Urban; and to the 49ers public relations department: Kirk Reynolds, Jason Jenkins, Kristin Johnson, Kristina Hartman, Fitz Ollison, Matt Kramer, and Ryan Moore. A special thanks to Cindy Krawczyk. I'd also like to acknowledge Glenn Dickey, Dave Newhouse, Dan McGuire, James D. Houston, and Bob Raissman, whose works helped light the way.

Nearly sixty former and current players and coaches were interviewed in the research phase, and I remain grateful that they were giving of their time and experiences.

Finally I'd like to thank my neighbor, Ron Imperiale, a 49ers aficionado who allowed me to use reference material from his extensive 49ers library.

# Sadness, Triumph, and Heartbreak

For all its simplicity and grace, the Alley-Oop pass is rooted, really, in desperation and happenstance. The seeds of the play made famous by the leaping grabs of 49ers receiver R. C. Owens were planted before the start of the 1957 season. Playing the Chicago Cardinals in the fourth of the team's six exhibition games, 49ers quarterback Y. A. Tittle found himself at midfield looking downfield for a receiver as he ran around, dodging a fierce pass rush. "I was planning to throw it away," Tittle said. But the ball slipped slightly from his grasp as he heaved it. The pass that he intended to throw beyond the end zone instead floated toward a mix of Cardinals and 49ers clustered around the goal line.

"R. C. was in the crowd and he went up, out-jumped everybody, and came down with the ball for a touchdown," Tittle said. "I told him after the game, 'You made me look like a hero.'"

"I can do it every time," replied Owens, a 6'3", 207-pound rookie from the College of Idaho who also had starred in basketball. "Good Lord," Tittle said. "If you can do it one out of three times, I'll take it, because that's a touchdown."

At least initially, though, Tittle and Owens viewed the play more or less as an accident and didn't press to refine it or add it to the 49ers playbook. It also didn't make an immediate impression on coach Frankie Albert, or his top assistant, Red Hickey. It would be rediscovered, however, after a painful season-opening loss to those same Cardinals.

Still fuming over the upset—Albert had predicted the 49ers would beat the "weaker" Cardinals in the days before the game—Hickey became even more exasperated with what he viewed as the players' lethargic preparations for the upcoming contest against the Los Angeles Rams. "He was just coming unglued," Owens recalled. "He said, 'How are our guys going to get any practice unless you throw the ball downfield?'"

The principal target of Hickey's ire was Tittle, who at the time was playing the role of Rams quarterback Norm Van Brocklin so his defensive teammates could get some sense of Los Angeles's deep-strike passing attack. Tittle at first was reluctant to pass downfield into a crowd because he figured no quarterback would make a throw that could be easily intercepted. "There's guys all over him," Tittle complained. An irritated Hickey bellowed, "I don't care how high you have to throw it, or how long. Just throw it in there. Give them a picture. Let them pursue to the ball."

So on the next play, Tittle threw a high, arching pass downfield to Owens, who pulled off a repeat of the acrobatic catch he made two months previously against the Cardinals. "There's two guys on me and I out-jumped them to make the catch," said Owens.

A moment later Owens made another leaping catch over a group of 49ers defenders, and then he made another and another. "I'll be damned," marveled rookie quarterback John Brodie, who stood nearby with Hickey and 49ers coach Frankie Albert.

"They're all over him—they're all over him and he's catching the ball," Tittle said.

"Coach," Tittle added to Albert, "if he's catching the ball like that, we ought to put that play in for the game against the Rams."

"Yeah, but what do we call it?" said Albert.

According to Owens, someone from the group made up of Tittle, Brodie, Albert, and Hickey blurted out, "That's our Alley-Oop play." Some accounts credit Hickey, though Owens can't say for sure who said it. No matter why, how, or who christened the play, the Alley-Oop would become part of the nation's football lexicon. The 49ers would see to that in short order.

The Rams were the darlings of Hollywood, a past champion and emerging as a chief rival of the 49ers, who were in their eighth NFL season after spending the first four years of their existence in the All-America Football Conference. A sellout crowd of 59,637 jammed Kezar Stadium to see the teams' first meeting of the year.

*49ers quarterback Frankie Albert (63) running against the Cleveland Browns in 1951.* AP

Wide receivers Clyde Conner and Billy Wilson teamed up for the 49ers' first touchdown. After a catch by Conner, he lateraled the ball to the trailing Wilson, who took it in for the score. That gave the 49ers, who earlier had a safety, a 9–7 lead.

In the final moments of the first half, Tittle called the Alley-Oop. Owens raced down the sideline, with Rams defensive back Don Burroughs running right alongside him. As they reached the end zone and turned back to look for the ball, Tittle lofted a pass that fluttered toward them. Both Burroughs and Owens jumped up for it, but it was Owens who came down with it for a 16–7 halftime lead.

The Rams used a pair of field goals and a 70-yard touchdown pass from Norm Van Brocklin to Leon Clarke to surge back in front, and that's the way it stayed until late in the game. With just over three minutes left, the 49ers advanced to the Rams 11 yard line, largely behind the running of Hugh McElhenny and Gene Babb. Tittle again called for the Alley-Oop. As Tittle dropped back to pass, Owens ran to the end zone, with defensive back Jesse Castete parked right in his hip pocket. Tittle let fly a soft, arcing pass, and Owens out-jumped Castete to pull it down in the end zone for the decisive touchdown in the 49ers' 23–20 victory.

An ecstatic Owens told Tittle afterward that they could make the acrobatic play a part of their routine. "Colonel," Owens said, referring to Tittle by one of his many nicknames, "throw it as high and as far as you want because I'll get to it. Just put a little wobble on it so I can catch it better." Tittle went along with the request, relying on the promise of more touchdowns to overcome his reluctance and embarrassment over fluttering his downfield throws to Owens.

The Alley-Oop's success was greeted with banner headlines in Bay Area newspapers, and the novel play occupied a prominent place in the 49ers playbook for years to come. It also was central to several cliff-hangers that followed its unveiling. None was more dramatic than the 41-yarder Owens caught in the final moments of a 35–31 victory over Detroit. Owens soared past Detroit defensive backs Jim David and Jack Christiansen, who would later become the 49ers head coach, for the winning touchdown. "It pulled us out of a lot of tight spots," said Hall of Fame running back Joe Perry, who remains the 49ers' all-time leading rusher. "R. C. could jump sky-high. He'd play it like he was going up for a rebound in basketball. Pretty soon, it became one of Tittle's favorite plays. Most of the time, it seemed to get us out of a pickle."

Even a failed Alley-Oop would sometimes work in favor of the 49ers. The week after the Rams game, the 49ers played George Halas's Bears at Chicago. With the Bears leading 17–14 in the late going, the 49ers defense, helped by key stops from Ed Henke and Charlie Powell, forced a Chicago punt. Tittle launched an Alley-Oop pass to the end zone for Owens that fell incomplete before connecting in succession with Hugh McElhenny, Clyde Conner, and Billy Wilson to move the 49ers to the Bears 7 yard line with just seconds remaining.

Again Tittle called for an Alley-Oop. But Chicago defenders cut Owens down at the line of scrimmage. The receiver managed to stagger into the end zone, turning around and falling to his knees as Tittle threw a pass to him low and hard. The ball zipped through the outstretched hands of Chicago defenders and into the arms of Owens, who cradled the ball for a 21–17 decision over the Bears. "I guess you can call that the 'Alley-Down' or my 'prayer pass,'" said Owens.

To the Bears, though, it was a fluke. They looked forward to reversing the outcome when they traveled to San Francisco in two weeks for their second meeting with what at least one Bears player described as the "worst team we've played all year."

R. C. Owens, the 49ers fabulous pass catcher, demonstrates his Alley-Oop catch for the camera. AP

Anthony J. Morabito was a San Francisco lumberman with a passion for football. Rebuffed initially by the NFL in a bid for a San Francisco franchise, Morabito and two partners formed the 49ers in 1946 as a charter member of the All-America Football Conference. Four years later, as part of a merger, the 49ers joined the NFL, fulfilling Morabito's long-shot dream.

Tragically, Morabito didn't live to see the 49ers make their first NFL playoff appearance. It was October 27, 1957, when the Chicago Bears traveled to San Francisco to play their second and final meeting of the season with the 49ers. Among the nearly 60,000 people in attendance at Kezar Stadium on that cold, gray day was Morabito, who watched from a suite as the 49ers fell behind 14–0 in the first quarter.

Tittle responded in the second quarter by leading the 49ers on a touchdown drive. During the Bears' ensuing possession, just as 49ers defensive tackle Bill Herchman broke through to take down Bears quarterback Ed Brown for a loss and force a punt, Morabito was convulsed by a massive heart attack.

Doctors began administering first aid even as a priest, who happened to be at the game, administered last rites. Lou Spadia, a front office staffer and later the 49ers general manager, said Morabito was carried down the stadium steps on a stretcher and rushed by ambulance to a hospital, where he was pronounced dead.

The players first noticed the press box commotion from the sideline and were informed at halftime by coach Frankie Albert that Morabito had been stricken. Word that the owner had died spread among the stunned and saddened group as the players resumed play in the third quarter, trailing the Bears 17–7. "Was it ever emotional," said Joe Perry, his voice cracking as he

## An Owner Passing

**The portrait of Anthony J. Morabito hangs in the den of Joe Perry's home in Chandler, Arizona. "Wherever I've been, that painting has always gone with me. It always will," said Perry, who was part of the 49ers' fabled "Million Dollar Backfield" in the 1950s with Y. A. Tittle, Hugh McElhenny, and John Henry Johnson.**

**"You've got to understand that Tony and I were like father and son from the get-go," Perry said. "From the first time we met, we kind of attached ourselves to each other. But that's the way he treated all his players. We were like family, and that's why we would give our all for him."**

recalled Morabito's death in an interview forty-seven years later. "You've never seen thirty-three of us players crying all at the same time."

"There was a lot of disbelief, and we were all kind of looking at each other," recalled Pro Football Hall of Fame tackle Bob St. Clair. "Damn it, we wanted to do something for Tony. No way were we going to lose that game. We knew we could win it, and we did."

With pass-rushing defensive tackle Leo Nomellini in the face of Brown, a pass by the Bears quarterback was intercepted and returned for a touchdown by fellow defensive tackle Bill Herchman, pulling the 49ers to 17–14. Then Dick Moegle picked off Brown early in the fourth quarter to set up the go-ahead touchdown drive. Perry hadn't played much because of a knee injury, but he pressed Albert to let him in the game. "I wanted to go in. I had to go in," said Perry, who contributed an 8-yard run on the decisive drive.

Tittle finished the march with an 11-yard touchdown pass to Billy Wilson, putting the 49ers in front early in the fourth quarter. The Bears drove deep into 49ers territory in the late going, but Moegle came up with his third interception of the day, allowing Tittle to take a knee and run out the clock. "Tony was one of those rare owners who had a strong relationship with his players, and the ballplayers cared for him, too," Tittle said. "We like to think that game was our gift to him, even though he was gone. We just played our hearts out for him."

Morabito was forty-seven when he died. His share of the team passed to his wife, Josephine. His brother, Vic, who also had a stake in the team, assumed day-to-day control.

The 49ers followed their emotional win over the Bears with a last-second triumph over the Detroit Lions on a long Alley-Oop from Tittle to Owens. The 35–31 win over the Lions on November 3, 1957, lifted San Francisco to a 5–1 mark and a 2-game lead in the Western Conference at the midway point of a twelve-game season.

Some tough times were looming, though. The 49ers opened a four-game road trip at Los Angeles, dropping a 37–24 decision to the Rams before a record crowd of 102,368. Subsequent losses at Detroit and Baltimore extended the skid to three games before the 49ers halted it by beating the New York Giants 27–17 at snow-covered Yankee Stadium.

Back at Kezar Stadium the following week, the 49ers faced a rematch with the Colts, who were a game in front of San Francisco, thanks to their victory two weeks earlier. Johnny Unitas's

Frank Albert, as 49ers coach, talks on the sidelines to overhead observers during a game in 1957. AP

72-yard touchdown pass to Lenny Moore gave the Colts a 13–10 lead in the third quarter and, with Baltimore's defense continually pounding Tittle, it looked like that might be enough. But the 49ers put together a drive in the last couple minutes, getting a 43-yard chunk when Hugh McElhenny turned a short pass into a big gainer that reached the Colts 15 yard line. Joe Perry made a catch for a 1-yard gain, but the next play went nowhere as Tittle was hurried into an incompletion.

Tittle was hit hard as he threw and couldn't continue, bringing on rookie quarterback John Brodie with less than a minute to play. After a third-down incompletion, Brodie told his teammates in the huddle, "Well, what do you guys want to do?"

"For some reason, I was the only one who opened my mouth," said McElhenny. "Usually I never do that, but that time I did. Nobody was saying anything, so I said, 'Hit me in the flat on a little out and up.' I do an out, he throws the ball to me, and we beat the Colts."

Brodie started the December 15 season finale against the Green Bay Packers, but with the 49ers trailing 20–10, he was relieved by Tittle, who rallied the team to a 27–20 victory. The win clinched the 49ers' first NFL postseason berth.

On that same day, the Rams upset the Colts 37–21 and Detroit beat the Chicago Bears 21–13, knocking Baltimore from the playoff picture. The Lions and 49ers tied for the Western Conference title, producing a divisional playoff between the two teams with the winner advancing to the NFL Championship Game. The playoff was at Kezar Stadium and it endures as the game that got away from the 49ers.

George Seifert's roots with the 49ers run deep. A 49ers assistant under Bill Walsh for ten years, he became the only native

# Agony and Ecstasy

The 49ers' stunning collapse to Detroit in the 1957 divisional playoff endures as one of the organization's greatest disappointments. The winning touchdown catch by Dwight Clark in the waning seconds of the 1981 NFC Championship Game against the Dallas Cowboys stands out as one of the team's great triumphs.

George Seifert was a witness to both. He was an usher at Kezar Stadium when the 49ers blew a 20-point, third-quarter lead in a 31–27 loss to Detroit. Twenty-four years later, he saw the 49ers beat Dallas 28–27 on Clark's catch from the press box, where he was working as an assistant coach for San Francisco. "To be at the low ebb and experience the heartbreak, and then years later to witness such a pivotal moment in the rise of the team was pretty exciting and something I'll always remember," Seifert said. "The contrast in emotions, that was the thing that struck me. Driving over to my mother-in-law's after we beat Dallas, it seemed like the whole city just erupted in celebration. People were climbing telephone poles, leaning out of their cars, just mad with joy. It was wild."

San Franciscan to coach the team when he succeeded Walsh in 1989. But back on December 22, 1957, the day the 49ers and Lions met in a divisional playoff, Seifert was a senior at San Francisco's Polytechnic High School working the game at Kezar Stadium as an usher.

In between helping people to their seats, Seifert watched as Tittle, after a fumble by Detroit quarterback Tobin Rote, threw a long, high pass to Owens for the 49ers' first touchdown. Moments later, Hugh McElhenny turned a short pass into a 47-

yard touchdown, and the 49ers were up 14–0. By halftime, after adding a pair of field goals by Gordy Soltau and a touchdown catch by Billy Wilson, the 49ers led 24–7. During the break, some players were so sure they were going to win they started making plans for how to spend their playoff bonus. "Everybody was talking about getting our ladies new furs," said wide receiver Billy Wilson.

On the first play of the second half, it looked like they could take that bonus money to the bank. McElhenny took a pitchout and swept around right end. He cut back to pick up a block from Clyde Conner and broke into the clear, going for 71 yards to Detroit's 9 yard line before being pushed out of bounds. But three subsequent runs by Joe Arenas, Perry, and McElhenny netted 6 yards, and the 49ers settled for another field goal by Soltau to put them up 27–7.

Right around then, Seifert recalls, one of his buddies bet another friend a hot dog that the 49ers would lose the game. The bet, Seifert said, was his friend's youthful attempt at reverse psychology because he really wanted the hometown team to win as badly as anyone. "But it seemed like almost from the moment that bet was made, the game began to unravel for the 49ers," Seifert said.

From confident and giddy and envisioning a berth in the upcoming championship game, the 49ers suddenly began to founder. "We were very happy that we had the game under control 24–7 at halftime," McElhenny said. "How in the hell are you going to blow that? I mean, we'd been beat before but we hadn't blown a lead like that. But we blew it. I can still remember [Lions fullback] Tom 'The Bomb' Tracy going right up the middle on us. Defensively, we just couldn't stop him."

A fumble by Tittle led to a Lions touchdown and, after Detroit forced a 49ers punt, Tracy broke loose on a 58-yard scoring run. After another 49ers punt, Gene Gedman had a short touchdown run to give the Lions a 28–27 lead early in the fourth quarter. Detroit added a field goal after Tittle threw an interception, and San Francisco's last-ditch drive ended when Tittle was intercepted for a third time. "I'm still trying to forget that game," Tittle said. "But I was the one calling the plays, and I take full responsibility for booting it away. We had such a good lead, I didn't see how they could beat us, so I started trying to ride the clock out by running the ball. But their defense stiffened up and got tougher and, unfortunately, Detroit came back with some big plays and won it."

Running back Joe Perry said the 49ers offense, which had been so effective in the first half, simply ground to a halt in the second half, allowing the Lions to catch up and overtake them. "What a blow that was to all of us," Perry said. "I'm still not sure how or why our offense came to a standstill. All I do know is that the harder we tried to get it going, the worse we got."

The defeat brought an agonizing end to a tumultuous season, and the frustration from the loss seemed to permeate the organization for years. Seifert still recalls shuffling out of Kezar and sensing the fog hanging over the dispersing crowd like a blanket of disappointment. "You know, it was a really gray day," Seifert said. "But what I remember is the quiet after the game, and how sullen it was. Thousands of people were walking out of the stadium. Everybody had their heads down, and the silence was just deafening. It was an eerie feeling."

It would take the 49ers thirteen years to reach the playoffs again, a span in which the team had four different head coaches.

# Beach Football

One of the casualties of the 49ers' playoff loss to Detroit was a week-long vacation to Puerto Vallarta that Y. A. Tittle, Matt Hazeltine, Billy Wilson, and Hugh McElhenny had planned to take with their anticipated bonus money. The four, along with their spouses, finally got around to taking the trip some fifteen years later. "Y. A. was the instigator," McElhenny said. "But we all had a good time."

During their stay, the players were tossing a football on the beach when a group of six college-age youths came along and challenged them to a game of touch football. To make the teams even, one of the youths joined the elder foursome. "He comes into the huddle—he doesn't know who we are—and he starts saying how well he plays football and that he'll be quarterback," Wilson said. "Then he tells Y. A., 'Okay, baldy, you go do a down and out and I'll try to hit you.' We all just started laughing, didn't say a word, and did what we were supposed to do."

After a couple incompletions, Wilson tells his younger teammate, "Okay, why don't you let the old guy throw the ball and you block?" Bam! Tittle started tossing one touchdown pass after another, taking turns hitting Wilson, Hazeltine, and McElhenny as they scorched their younger opponents on their makeshift sandy field.

"I'll tell you, we were having a lot of fun, though we did beat them pretty bad," Wilson said. "They were kind of shocked and wondering how we did it. We finally told them who we were. They got a kick out of it."

And in a way, so did the four of them. They got to take their trip at long last and, this time, they won the game.

In that same period, the 49ers never had more than 7 wins in a season. Then, under Dick Nolan in 1970, the 49ers went 10–3–1 to win their first NFC West title in their final year at Kezar. The next season they would be playing in Candlestick Park.

# The Ghosts of Kezar

Coach Dick Nolan and his wife, Ann, walked away together from empty and quiet Kezar Stadium, still overwhelmed by thoughts of the 49ers' near-miss. Hours earlier, the Dallas Cowboys had hung on to beat the 49ers 17–10 in the NFC Championship Game on January 3, 1971, stamping one last defeat on the team's roller-coaster, twenty-five-year stay at Kezar.

As if seeing the 49ers get tripped up a step short of the Super Bowl in their final game at Kezar wasn't bad enough, the Nolans returned to find their car, parked on a nearby side street, surrounded by other parked vehicles. Nolan tried to maneuver out of the jam but couldn't get through. As he and his wife talked and wondered what to do, a small crowd gathered, and a few of them recognized Nolan as the 49ers coach. Before Nolan could say, "Wait till next year," eight to twelve of them got together and lifted the couple's car into the clear. "They picked my car up and moved it to where it had to go so I could get out," Nolan said years later. "And they set it down nice and easy. I'm glad they did because if they hadn't, I might still be there. It was a surprise. That was after a loss, but then they were just happy to see us get into the playoffs against anybody."

For many years after the 49ers left their funky home in the heart of the city for Candlestick Park, their base for five Super Bowl titles, there had been little acknowledgment of the team's colorful Kezar Stadium past. Built in the 1920s, the 59,000-seat, bleacher-lined stadium was nestled amid the damp and the fog on the edge of Golden Gate Park. The 49ers began calling it home in 1946, the first year of their existence, and it was there that the team's fans were introduced to such greats as Y. A. Tittle, Joe Perry, Hugh McElhenny, Bob St. Clair, and Leo Nomellini.

Demolished in 1989 because of earthquake damage, Kezar today is a lively shadow of itself. Reconfigured as a 10,000-seat stadium with a year-round track surrounding the football field, Kezar continues to host high school football and soccer games and other events and as always remains the traditional province of fog and seagulls. The 49ers have even reconnected with their former home, staging an annual public practice at the new Kezar and in the process reviving the memories that keep the old Kezar

# Jim Marshall's Wrong-Way Run

Bob Fouts remembers it as the darnedest sight in his twenty-two years as a 49ers broadcaster. During a 1964 game at Kezar Stadium, Minnesota defensive lineman Jim Marshall scooped up a fumble by 49ers quarterback Billy Kilmer and ran 66 yards—to the wrong end zone. Fouts said, "I can still see Vikings coach Norm Van Brocklin running down the sideline and waving his arms, trying to get his attention that he was going the wrong way."

Marshall had broken through the protection and was in the midst of a twisting, wild backfield chase of Kilmer when he got turned around right before picking up the loose ball. As he ran toward the end zone, guard Bruce Bosley trailed behind him. "Bosley was chasing him, thinking any minute he's going to turn around and he could whack him," 49ers tackle Bob St. Clair said.

That didn't happen. Marshall reached the end zone and tossed the ball away in celebration, thinking he'd scored a touchdown. In reality, it was a safety—the longest in NFL history—for the 49ers. "That a baby! Thank you so much," Bosley told the flabbergasted Marshall, giving him a quick handshake.

As it turned out, Marshall's wrong-way run, while memorable, didn't hurt the Vikings. They still beat the 49ers, 27–22.

alive. "Every opposition team that ever played there hated it, but we loved the place," St. Clair said.

St. Clair had a special bond, having played at Kezar in high school, college, and the pros.

While playing for San Francisco's Polytechnic High School, Bob St. Clair scored a touchdown on a tackle-eligible play. "Five guys were hanging onto me, and I dragged them into the end zone," St. Clair recalled.

A couple of years later, as an end for the University of San Francisco, he caught a pass from Ed Brown and bolted down the sideline. As he neared the goal line, St. Mary's John Henry Johnson, under a full head of steam, smashed into him from the side. The 6'9" St. Clair flipped in the air and came crashing down on his back. "I had seen him coming out of the corner of my eye and figured I'd run over him, but he hit me full speed, his shoulder and helmet getting me right on the thigh," St. Clair said. "It lifted me way up into the air and the landing wasn't pretty. I'd never been hit so hard in my life. It knocked me out of the game."

As a tackle for the 49ers during a game in the mid-1950s, he and teammate Leo Nomellini pulled off a looping stunt while rushing a punt. St. Clair charged up the middle unblocked, stuffing the kick and catching the punter's foot full in the mouth. "I spit out five of my front teeth," St. Clair said. "I stuffed some cotton in my mouth and kept playing."

All of those episodes serve to illustrate St. Clair's extraordinary connection to Kezar. Indeed, no player is more closely associated with San Francisco's quirky stadium. St. Clair played all his home games at Kezar during high school and college and in his eleven-year career with the 49ers. That amounted to 189 games over seventeen years on the Kezar field that now bears his name.

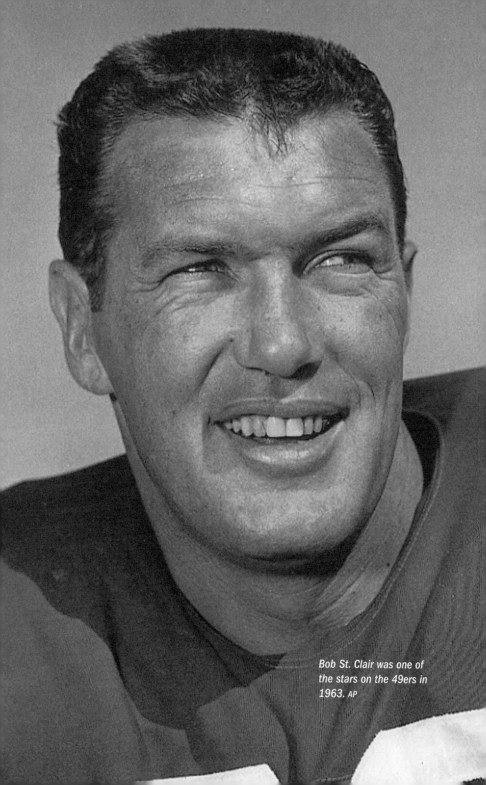

Bob St. Clair was one of the stars on the 49ers in 1963. AP

But for all the glory and thrills, heartache and pain, cheers and, yes, boos, that came his way, the moment he gets the biggest kick out of revolved around a pratfall that brought a packed house at Kezar down—in laughter. As the first player introduced before a game in 1959, he tripped and fell over a slight rise while running full speed onto the field. Tittle was supposed to have gone first, but he knew the fans were upset with his recent play and he didn't want to be showered with boos, so the quarterback begged St. Clair to go instead. "Okay, I'll take the heat for you," St. Clair said he told Tittle. "Well, I took a tumble headlong into the end zone and everyone in that stadium started laughing. They were still laughing when Y. A. was introduced, so he got away with it."

Pro Football Hall of Fame fullback Joe Perry has his own Kezar memories, too. But before that, even before he gained a yard for the 49ers, Perry had earned himself a nickname: "Joe the Jet."

Signed in 1948 while the 49ers were still part of the All-America Football Conference (AAFC), Perry had a knack for bolting out of his stance. He put his quick starts on display during the team's training camp practices at Menlo College, to the initial annoyance of quarterback Frankie Albert. "We had a trap play that was going to me, but by the time Frankie turned around to give me the ball, I'd be 5 yards by him," Perry said. "He says, 'You're cheatin'.' I tell him, 'No, I'm not.' You see, he was used to a big, lumbering fullback. Hell, I wanted to get through that hole."

An exasperated Albert called the play four or five more times, but Perry still was blowing by him before he could stick the ball in the fullback's belly. Finally, 49ers coach Buck Shaw stepped in and suggested Perry take a small jab step before accelerating toward the hole. At the same time, Albert made a point of quickening his own footwork to reach the point where he could hand off to Perry. The two finally began to connect, but Albert still marveled aloud, "Joe, you're just like one of those jets flying around up there."

"That just stuck, and so I became 'Joe the Jet,'" Perry said, "because Frankie couldn't get around fast enough to get me the ball. Isn't it great to be young?"

It's even better when you're young and good, as Perry showed the first time he touched the ball in a game for the 49ers. San Francisco was playing host to Buffalo in the AAFC opener at Kezar when Albert called a pitchout to Perry. The 6', 200-pounder took the toss, sailed around end, and outran Buffalo's defenders for a 58-yard touchdown as part of the 49ers' 35–14 victory. "They had no idea I had the speed that I had," said Perry, who once ran the 100-yard dash in 9.7 seconds while in high school in Los Angeles. "From there, everything just kind of blossomed."

Perry continued his standout play after the 49ers joined the NFL in 1950, becoming the first player in the league's history to run for 1,000 yards in consecutive seasons in 1953 and 1954. A cornerstone in the 49ers' "Million Dollar Backfield" that also included fellow Hall of Famers Y. A. Tittle, Hugh McElhenny, and John Henry Johnson, Perry remains the leading rusher in 49ers history with 7,344 yards. He also ran for 1,345 yards in his two seasons with the team while it was in the AAFC.

For all his on-field accomplishments, Perry also is remembered as the 49ers' first black player, a signing that paved the way for some of the team's greatest stars. The 49ers were still in the AAFC, in the third year of their existence, when owner Anthony Morabito moved to acquire Perry.

A World War II veteran, Perry was playing for a navy team at the Alameda Naval Air Station when Morabito first saw him in

# Picking Up the Tab

Hugh McElhenny found out right away there was no free lunch in the NFL. The eighth overall pick by the 49ers in 1952, he was summoned to a meeting at the Sheraton Hotel in Los Angeles with team co-owner Vic Morabito. "We were out in the patio by the pool having lunch," McElhenny says. "And he says, 'Hugh, what do you think you deserve?'"

McElhenny responded by asking for $30,000, a figure suggested to him by Frankie Albert. Morabito was aghast at the request, telling McElhenny it was absurd. Instead, he offered a contract for $5,000. "I said, no, I don't think so," McElhenny said, adding he just might go play in Canada.

The two talked a little more, ate lunch, and McElhenny says Morabito then excused himself from the table. "I thought he was going to the john, but wherever he went, he didn't come back, and I got stuck with the bill. That was my introduction to the 49ers," McElhenny said with a laugh.

Eventually, the 49ers bumped up their offer to $7,000 and McElhenny, with some encouragement from his wife, Peggy, signed the contract.

1947. He scouted Perry on the recommendation of former 49ers offensive lineman John Woudenberg, who was helping to coach the base's team. Perry put on a stunning display that foreshadowed the fleet, powerful running style that characterized his pro career. He carried the ball four times, scoring each time. His shortest run: 55 yards.

After seeing Perry practically duplicate the feat in a second game, Morabito told him he'd like him to play for the 49ers the next season, when his navy tour was up. Perry agreed without hesitation. "We shook hands, and that's how I started playing for the 49ers, on a handshake, not a contract," he said.

Integration of professional sports was just beginning when Perry joined the 49ers before the 1948 season. Running back Kenny Washington and end Woody Strode became the first black players in the NFL's modern era when they signed with the Los Angeles Rams in 1946. Later that same year, guard Bill Willis and running back Marion Motley joined the AAFC's Cleveland Browns. Jackie Robinson went on to break baseball's color barrier in 1947 when he was signed by the Brooklyn Dodgers. Through it all, Perry and Morabito forged an extraordinarily close relationship, one that helped Perry get through some of the hard times that came with being a trail blazer in an intensely physical, competitive sport. Recalling the counsel of his friend and team owner, Perry said, "Tony told me, 'Listen, you know you're going to get a lot of abuse. Not only are you going to get it physically out on the field, you're going to hear language that you're not going to care for. But you know you're going to have to ride with it. You're going to have to bite the bullet.'

"I said 'Tony, I have no problem with that. You can't hurt me with words. You can't hurt me by calling me a name. You just make me come back at you that much harder.' That's what used to happen all the time in games. A guy would say, 'You'd better not come back through here, you n—.' I said, 'I'll be right back,' and I'd come back that much harder. That's the way I played. That's how I dealt with it. I could care less what you called me, but you had to put the leather on me to stop me.

"Tony said, 'That's what I want to hear.' I said, 'You don't have to worry about me going crazy because somebody's calling me something.' For years it went that way, and we never had a problem. Now, it was a different story if you kicked me while I was down. I'd come up swinging then."

Hardy Brown, a diminutive linebacker for the 49ers, also packed a wallop. A member of the 49ers from 1951 to 1955, Brown developed a hit alternately known as a "hump block" or "shoulder tackle." Strong, fast, and absolutely fearless, Brown disdained the traditional "stick-and-wrap" technique in favor of launching himself head-and-shoulders first into a ball carrier. Often, he'd catch a runner right under his chin, stopping him cold and maybe knocking him out cold, too. "It was almost like he was a missile," said Bob Fouts, who called 49ers games on radio and television for more than twenty years. "He'd be flying through the air hitting people."

There was a downside to his novel tackling technique. Sometimes he'd miss. "Players were always looking out for him because they didn't want to get nailed," recalled former New York Giants defensive back Dick Nolan, a contemporary of Brown and later the 49ers coach. "He'd use that hump block and if he hit you, he'd knock you into the next county. The thing is, if he missed, you'd be gone."

In the 1953 season opener against Philadelphia at Kezar, Brown didn't miss. His bone-rattling hit on Toy Ledbetter knocked the Eagles running back out cold and out of the game during the first half. Tension between the teams was simmering in the aftermath of the devastating hit, and it soon would erupt into an all-out brawl that came to be called "The Donnybrook." The third-quarter free-for-all was triggered after 49ers defensive end Charlie Powell and Eagles lineman Bobby Walter got into a punching match near midfield.

Players from both teams rushed onto the field. At one point, 49ers Hugh McElhenny had one arm wrapped around the Eagles Pete Pihos in a headlock and used the other to fend off another Eagles player by swinging his helmet toward him. "I was holding onto him and just trying to keep other people away," McElhenny said. "And we were backpedaling down toward the west end zone. That's where the 49ers band was. Pretty soon, they were out on the field fighting with us and helping us out." Before joining the fray, the 49ers band played the national anthem in a futile attempt to calm the situation.

Finally, the officials, along with a contingent of San Francisco police that had come onto the field, restored order. Fans were shooed back to their seats, the musicians-turned-fighters went back to their end zone stand, and the players returned to the sideline that they shared. The 49ers wound up winning the game, 31–21. As for the winner of The Donnybrook, the jury's still out.

There's no question about the man who would be king, though. Hugh "the King" McElhenny came on the Kezar scene because of a phone call in the dead of night. When coach Buck Shaw answered, he was greeted by the excited voice of his quarterback, Frankie Albert. "I've just seen the best running back in my life, and you've got to draft him," Albert told Shaw. Albert had been among the professional players playing in the 1952 Hula Bowl against a group of college all-stars, and McElhenny was the running back he was talking about. Shaw was anxious to act on Albert's advice. His only concern was that McElhenny would be taken before he could exercise the 49ers' eighth overall pick in the draft. When McElhenny was still there, Shaw grabbed the former University of Washington star with the 49ers' top draft pick in 1952.

# Worming Their Way through Kezar

Fog and wind weren't the only elements of Mother Nature to grace Kezar Stadium. There were times when the field was crawling with, well, night crawlers. "If a guy was tackled and driven into the ground, he'd be liable to be eating worms," 49ers broadcaster Bob Fouts said.

Jim Shofner, a 49ers assistant coach in the late 1960s and 1970s, recalled the slithery critters were especially prevalent before a 1969 game against the Rams. "The field was just covered with worms," Shofner said. A friend of his on the Rams, linebacker Maxie Baughan, "was picking them up and throwing them at me. I mean, you couldn't take a step on that field without coming across worms."

The fast, elusive McElhenny would make an impression the first time he played for the 49ers. He, along with second-round pick tackle Bob Toneff from Notre Dame, had joined the team the day before the 49ers were to host the Chicago Cardinals in an exhibition game at Kezar. After getting fitted for uniforms and helmets, the two plopped on the bench expecting they'd watch their first game from the sideline and ease into action the next time around. Albert, who called the shots on the team as much as Shaw did, had other ideas. "All of a sudden, in the third or fourth quarter, Frankie called a time-out, walked over, and told Shaw to put me in," McElhenny said. "Buck says, 'He doesn't know the plays.' 'That's okay. Just put him in,' Frankie says."

"So we get in the huddle, and we all kind of get down on our knees and Frankie is drawing the play on the ground, just like

*Hugh McElhenny (39) turns the corner against the Los Angeles Rams at Kezar Stadium in 1955.* AP

sandlot football. He says, 'Hugh, just swing out here, Leo [Nomellini], you pull. Billy Wilson, you block down,' and so forth. It basically was a 49 toss, and I go 42 yards for a touchdown. That was the first time I touched the ball for the 49ers."

It would certainly not be the last. Far from it. A master of improvisation who became known as "The King," McElhenny developed into the greatest broken-field runner of his day. He combined speed with elusiveness and defied tacklers, gaining

# Twisting and Turning

It wasn't Hugh McElhenny's longest run, maybe not even the prettiest, but it was the most breathtaking. Traded to the expansion Vikings in 1961 after run-ins with then San Francisco coach Red Hickey, the thirty-two-year-old McElhenny was playing his old team for the first time in an October game at Minnesota.

On the old Statue of Liberty play, Fran Tarkenton dropped back as if to pass and then handed the ball to McElhenny, who embarked on a remarkable 32-yard scoring run in which he seemingly dodged the entire 49ers defense. The run included so many twists and turns, feints and cuts that the distance covered probably was two or three times more than the actual yardage. "As many as 9 shots were made to tackle me, and they missed," McElhenny said. "I remember getting around Leo Nomellini first. Matt Hazeltine missed me twice. So did Eddie Dove. Jerry Mertens missed me." Some of his former 49ers teammates who witnessed the play from the sideline were so impressed by the run that they began applauding.

The Vikings coach at the time, Norm Van Brocklin, told writer Dave Newhouse years later that McElhenny's amazing change-of-direction jaunt through the 49ers defense "was the greatest run I ever saw. Whenever I think something's impossible, I put that film on the projector and watch it again."

running room in tight situations with uncanny, sometimes repeated cutbacks. "I didn't like to go over by the sidelines, so I'd come back against the grain because they would all be off balance," McElhenny said. "As I came back, I could always pick up Gordy Soltau on one side or Billy Wilson on the other or Leo Nomellini or Bob St. Clair.

"Gale Sayers, he was a glider, and I would say I was a glider, too. It's just a fear, not of getting hurt, but of getting caught. I'd liken it to running down an alley, which is something I'd do when I was a kid. There was an alley in the back of our house. And there was a light at the end of it where the store was. I'd keep my eye on that and I'd just run for it, ducking and dodging around the areas where you'd get the feeling somebody might be hiding and jump out at you.

"It's a feeling. You can teach guys to run straight and strong and to know your assignments, but you can't teach guys like Barry Sanders, Gale Sayers, the really good open-field runners. You just can't teach it. No way. It's just a feel. Some kids have it and some kids don't. Basically a good running back will find daylight. That's the thing, finding that little crack."

Foreshadowing his Hall of Fame career, McElhenny shook free for runs of 89 and 82 yards in 1952. His sensational rookie campaign also included a 94-yard punt return that helped the 49ers beat the Chicago Bears for the first time in four tries since coming into the NFL in 1950. Both of the long touchdown runs were against the Dallas Texans, the latter coming at Kezar. McElhenny also broke loose for an 86-yard touchdown run against the Packers in Green Bay in 1956.

The epic runs from scrimmage endure as three of the four longest in the team's history. They're topped only by Garrison Hearst's 96-yard game-winning touchdown run to beat the New York Jets in overtime in the 1998 season opener.

# Groundwork for Greatness

In the midst of a 49ers road trip, coach Red Hickey gathered his players at a closed practice field at Georgetown University in Washington, D.C., and unveiled his plans for a radical new offense. The meeting came just a few days before the 49ers were to play the Baltimore Colts. "Guys," Hickey said, "I've got something here. It's the Shotgun, and here's how it goes."

On a chalkboard, Hickey outlined the novel formation for his players. The quarterback, he noted, lined up 4 or 5 yards deep in the backfield instead of being directly behind the center. Running backs and receivers were aligned on either side or positioned at a slight angle just in front of the quarterback. Center Frank Morze would be required to make a deeper snap to the quarterback. The scheme was akin to the old Single Wing, in which the ball could be snapped directly to the tailback. But in the Shotgun, the quarterback was still calling the shots, so to speak. He was just as likely to take off running or hand the ball off to one or two or three flanking backs as to throw a pass to a receiver out in the flat, over the middle, or down the field.

Variations of the Shotgun commonly used by NFL teams today are rooted in the pioneering 49ers offense. Hickey first used it November 27, 1960, against the befuddled Colts, who lost 30–22 to the underdog 49ers. San Francisco wide receiver R. C. Owens said that the Colts weren't sure how to adjust when quarterback John Brodie lined up in the backfield to accept the hike. "We hit 'em by surprise," said Owens, who had 6 catches for 148 yards and a touchdown before scoring the decisive touchdown on a lateral from tight end Dee Mackey. "They hadn't seen us run it. We were using it at different times and usually when we were moving the ball, it was with the Shotgun."

The Colts weren't the only ones unsure of what to make of the 49ers' radical formation. In the official play-by-play of the game, statisticians first referred to Brodie's depth in the backfield as being part of a Single Wing formation. Later they wrote that Brodie and Y. A. Tittle were passing or running from "a short punt formation."

Whenever the 49ers lined up against their defense in the Shotgun at practice, they could expect to hear ribbing from the

# Trade Deficit

For all of Hall of Fame quarterback Y. A. Tittle's success in San Francisco, Red Hickey viewed him as a poor fit in the Shotgun, and the coach was determined to trade him. He dealt him to the Giants in 1961, a deal that endures as one of the worst in 49ers history. Tittle, then thirty-four, was shipped to New York in exchange for their top draft pick, guard Lou Cordileone.

Tittle became the toast of New York, leading the Giants to the NFL Championship Game three straight times. Cordileone lasted only one season with the 49ers before being let go and finishing his career in New Orleans.

Cordileone later ran a bar in the city's French Quarter called The Huddle. In it he displayed a helmet that commemorated his link to the famed quarterback with the words, TRADED FOR Y. A. TITTLE.

team's great defensive tackle, Leo Nomellini. "Uh, oh, they're going to the water pistol," he often said, laughing.

"People thought I was being goofy," Hickey said. "Well, if it works, you aren't so goofy. I was convinced that the offense we had just wasn't good enough [to beat the league's best teams]," Hickey added. "So I started playing around with some ideas in my head. I wanted to have something that could confuse them, keep other teams guessing, and by golly, that's what the Shotgun seemed to do."

The 49ers won four of their last five games in 1960 while principally using the Shotgun. They committed to it fully at the start of the next season, after Hickey used one of the team's three first-round picks on UCLA's Billy Kilmer, the running quarter-back he felt he needed to give the Shotgun legs. The addition of Kilmer allowed Hickey to operate a three-quarterback shuffle. Brodie remained the focal point on passing downs, Kilmer was the principal rushing threat, and Bobby Waters was viewed as the dual purpose quarterback, solid as a runner and passer.

The rotation made the Shotgun all the more difficult to defend, at least at first, and the 49ers stormed to a 4–1 start in 1961. The run included two startling victories in successive weeks—a 49–0 rout of Detroit at Tiger Stadium and a 35–0 drubbing of the rival Los Angeles Rams at Kezar Stadium.

The 49ers stunned the Lions with a quarterback rotation that included a different one on each of their first three plays. The opening sequence included a 31-yard sweep by Kilmer that led to a touchdown. During the 49ers' next series, Brodie completed a 45-yard pass to Clyde Conner, Kilmer twice swept around end for gains of 12 and 10 yards, and Waters, behind a Brodie block, went in untouched around the left side for a 1-yard touchdown. "We were killing guys," Owens said. "We were the talk of the football world."

Hickey remembers his friend, Detroit coach George Wilson, coming up to him after the 49ers had handed the Lions one of the worst losses in their history. "You red-headed bastard. What are you pulling on me here?" Wilson demanded.

"Well, George, I had a hard time beating you, so I had to think of something new," Hickey replied.

But the 49ers would only be able to take opposing teams by surprise for so long. The novelty of the Shotgun crashed to a halt midway through the season at Chicago. George Halas's Bears, anticipating the plays out of the Shotgun because of tendencies established over the first five games, would be at the right place at the right time to stop the 49ers' attack cold. Chicago routed San Francisco 31–0. The Pittsburgh Steelers followed the Bears' model in beating the 49ers 20–10 the next week, and even Detroit wasn't fooled the second time around, tying the 49ers 20–20.

With injuries piling up and the Shotgun's effectiveness suddenly in question, the 49ers returned to a traditional pro-set offense, and Brodie became the primary quarterback during the final weeks of the 1961 campaign. Owens also finished strong, ending the year with 55 catches for 1,032 yards, the first receiver in the team's history to reach the yardage milestone.

The Shotgun resurfaced occasionally up until Hickey resigned three games into the 1963 season. But for nearly forty years after that, the 49ers pretty much put the scheme into mothballs. Brodie never really cared for it. Neither Joe Montana nor Steve Young, the team's top quarterbacks in the 1980s and 1990s, liked the Shotgun. They stayed away from it because they believed the formation made it too hard to read defenses and had an adverse effect on the timing-based West Coast offense installed by coach Bill Walsh.

But the Shotgun was revived by the 49ers in spot situations with Jeff Garcia and Tim Rattay, among others, embracing the notion of a backfield setup for the quarterback. It remains an effective means to counter an intense pass rush and offers opportunities for spread formations that can also open up lanes for runners and receivers alike.

# Joining the NFL's Elite

Jack Christiansen, a Hall of Fame defensive back for Detroit, famously pounded the end zone grass in frustration when Owens caught a last-second Alley-Oop pass over him to beat the Lions in a 1957 game at Kezar Stadium. The moment epitomized Christiansen's equally frustrating tenure as the 49ers coach, a nearly five-year run that ended after a 7–7 campaign in 1967. During his stay, the 49ers never finished a season more than half a game over .500.

Early on in his search for a new coach to replace Christiansen, Lou Spadia, the team's chief executive and a minority owner, focused on Dick Nolan, a former New York Giants defensive back who was working in Dallas as Cowboys coach Tom Landry's defensive coordinator. After having dinner with Nolan at San Francisco's Jack Tar Hotel, Spadia turned to his prospective coach and said, "Hey, is there any reason why I shouldn't hire you?"

"No, I'm perfectly fine. I'm the right man for the job," Nolan replied. "I just know I can build a team."

That was all Spadia needed to hear. "Okay, you're hired," he said.

Quiet and unassuming, but intense, Nolan first settled a festering quarterback controversy by endorsing John Brodie as the starter after a training camp competition with George Mira. Key players were added on both sides of the ball through the draft. Center Forrest Blue, linebacker Skip Vanderbundt, and defensive end Tommy Hart joined the 49ers in Nolan's first draft. Tight end Ted Kwalick, wide receiver Gene Washington, and linebacker Bob Hoskins were part of the 1969 draft, and defensive end

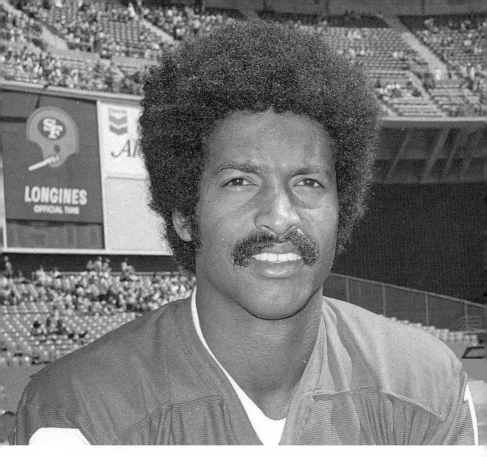

*Gene Washington was a key acquisition in the 1969 draft.* AP

Cedrick Hardman, cornerback Bruce Taylor, and running backs Vic Washington and Larry Schreiber were selected in 1970.

All of those players would become integral to the 49ers' 10–3–1 campaign in 1970 and to the team's first NFC West championship. It became clear the 49ers were on to something special a month into the 1970 season, when they registered their first win over the Los Angeles Rams in three years. Brodie touched off the 20–6 victory with a 12-yard touchdown run on a quarterback draw. "He walked in," tackle Cas Banaszek recalled. "There wasn't a guy within a mile of him."

A dominating 38–7 victory in the season finale against the Oakland Raiders (this was the first regular-season meeting between the regional rivals) clinched the NFC West title and returned the 49ers to the playoffs for the first time since 1957. It would be the first of three straight postseason trips by the 49ers, the greatest run of success the team would see until the fabled Bill Walsh teams of the 1980s.

## A Day at the Beach in Icy Minnesota

The 49ers had the look of a team playing mind games with their opponent. With the game-time temperature at Minnesota's Metropolitan Stadium hovering at 8 degrees, the 49ers trotted out in their short-sleeve jerseys to play a Vikings team that certainly had more time to get acclimated to the frigid weather than these fog-bound beach boys.

In actuality the 49ers had their short-sleeve jerseys on because those were the only ones they had to wear that day. At least the 49ers were allowed to use sideline heaters to warm up during the course of the game. Minnesota coach Bud Grant frowned on sideline blowers, and some Vikings players seeking warmth had to sneak toward the 49ers' bench, which at Metropolitan Stadium was on the same side of the field as that of the Vikings. "Grant wanted them to be tough guys," 49ers tackle Cas Banaszek said. "We had the blowers, hot towels, and a balm that we rubbed on to protect our skin. So we were handling the cold just fine, absolutely no problem. Those guys were freezing. We could see some of them inching toward our heaters and we'd tell them, 'Stay away!'"

# Mrs. Morabito

In the aftermath of the 49ers' first NFL playoff victory at frigid Minnesota, the jubilation was rampant in the locker room. "I was down there, too, jumping for joy along with everybody else," said 49ers president and general manager Lou Spadia. Suddenly, Spadia stopped celebrating. He remembered that team owner Josephine Morabito, who held the biggest stake in the team following the 1957 death of her husband, was sitting on a team bus all by herself. At the time, women were prohibited from being in the locker room.

"I thought I'd better go out there and see how she's doing," Spadia said. "So she tells me, 'For the first time in my life, I wish I could be a man, so I could be in that dressing room with our team.' Here, the owner missed out on all the great joy that was going on in there. I really think that's probably one of the reasons Mrs. Morabito decided to sell the team."

The Morabito family sold its controlling interest in the team to the DeBartolo family in 1977 for $17.5 million. A nephew of founder Anthony Morabito still holds a stake in the team.

Still, the game didn't begin well for the 49ers. Minnesota safety Paul Krause scooped up a fumble and returned it for a touchdown. There was no panicking by the 49ers, however. Brodie resolutely led a drive that he finished with a 24-yard touchdown pass to Dick Witcher. Then Bruce Gossett's field goal gave the 49ers a 10–7 lead.

With just under two minutes left, the 49ers were positioned for the clinching touchdown just outside the Vikings 1 yard line.

Inside the 49ers' huddle, players were alternately giddy and combative. Running back Doug Cunningham, whose burst had brought the ball nearly to the goal line, was yelling at Vikings linebacker Wally Hilgenberg. Fullback Ken Willard shouted at Cunningham to cool it. Brodie was having trouble calling a play over all the commotion. Finally, right guard Woody Peoples, who hardly ever said a word in the huddle, piped up. "Everybody, quiet!" Peoples snapped. "John," he told his quarterback, "run it over me."

Brodie responded by calling his first quarterback sneak in five years, following Peoples's devastating block into the end zone. The score stood up for the game-winner despite a late touchdown by the Vikings. San Francisco won 17–14. "That was a great win for us," Nolan said. "After it was over and we had beaten them, it was just overwhelming. I thought I'd be dead before we ever did something like that."

The 49ers followed their first NFL playoff victory with a narrow, 17–10 loss to the Dallas Cowboys, ending their season one victory shy of their first Super Bowl. "Dallas always gave us a hard time because, in my opinion, they had the best defense in football," said 49ers offensive coach Jim Shofner.

Their offense wasn't bad either. Duane Thomas ran for 143 yards including a 13-yard go-ahead score. "We couldn't stop him," tackle Len Rohde said. "But maybe we should have scored more points. That would have helped, too."

## Heartbreak Hill

With the 49ers taking a 28–13 lead into the fourth quarter of a 1972 divisional playoff game against Dallas, San Francisco

Quarterback John Brodie gave the 49ers an effective air attack in the 1960s.
Sports Gallery/Al Messerschmidt

seemed on course to reverse its playoff losses to the Cowboys in each of the previous two years. Certainly there was no sense of alarm when Toni Fritsch kicked a fourth-quarter field goal pulling the Cowboys to within 28–16. With the clock ticking down, 49ers tackle Len Rohde even remembered looking up to see the stands at Candlestick Park starting to empty. "A lot of people were leaving the stadium, like, 'We had it. Yeah! It was over,'" said Rhode. There was just one problem. It was far from over.

With 90 seconds left, Dallas quarterback Roger Staubach passed 20 yards to Billy Parks for a touchdown. The Cowboys' subsequent onside kick wasn't handled by Preston Riley, and Mel Renfro covered it for the Cowboys. A few seconds later, Ron Sellers caught the go-ahead touchdown pass. Dallas won 30–28 and again foiled the 49ers' bid to advance in the playoffs. "That last one," said quarterbacks and receivers coach Jim Shofner, "basically was just one of those crushing defeats."

No one took it harder than Riley, who never again played for the 49ers. "He was distraught," Banaszek said. "I roomed with him one year, and he was a very fragile guy. He just didn't handle it well, kind of went off the deep end. But it wasn't his fault. So they got one onside kick. Why didn't we stop them? They went in like we weren't even out there playing."

Nolan still laments what could have been, though he doesn't let himself dwell on it for too long. "We should have won one title in there somewhere," he said. "But you can't worry about that now. That's all woulda, shoulda, coulda."

With the team's core returning intact, the 49ers hoped to put aside the devastating loss to Dallas and renew their championship chase. They opened the 1973 campaign at Miami against the Dolphins, who had concluded a perfect season the year before. Playing in hot, muggy conditions, the 49ers took a 13–6 lead in the third quarter. But Steve Spurrier had come on in the second half for John Brodie, who was among several players sidelined for parts of the game due to heat prostration. The Dolphins rallied to score 15 fourth-quarter points and overtake the 49ers for a 21–13 victory.

Banaszek said he believes that grueling opener, even more than the hangover from the Dallas playoff loss, dragged the 49ers back into mediocrity. "That game just killed us," he said. "We had to land our plane in Chicago on the way home because we had three guys on board who needed to be hospitalized because of heat problems. Heck, I lost twenty-five pounds of water weight playing in that game. We just had a hard time recovering from it, really for the rest of the season."

The 49ers finished the 1973 campaign at 5–9, starting a string of eight straight non-playoff seasons. They would have six coaches and an ownership change before finally qualifying for the postseason again in 1981 under Bill Walsh. The return to the playoffs started an unprecedented round of success that would take the team to the pinnacle of the NFL, and keep it there for years.

# Dawn of a Dynasty

The first time Bill Walsh was approached about becoming the San Francisco 49ers head coach, he didn't take the job. That initial feeler came in a phone call from his friend, Raiders owner Al Davis, who had given Walsh his first job in the NFL in 1966 as the Raiders offensive backfield coach. Walsh had just finished a successful season as Stanford's head coach when Davis, acting as a go-between for San Francisco's new owners, the Edward J. DeBartolo family, and the general manager, Joe Thomas, inquired about his interest in the 49ers' job. For Walsh, the timing was wrong. Walsh said he was wary of the tumult he had seen around the 49ers in the first year of the DeBartolos' ownership and was put off by Thomas's abrasive style of management. "The 49ers were a franchise in trouble," Walsh said.

Monte Clark, a popular and successful coach, had been let go following the DeBartolos' purchase of the team from the Morabito family in a $17.5 million deal that was brokered by Davis. Clark's successor, Ken Meyer, lasted only a year, going 5–9 in the NFL's last fourteen-game season before being fired.

Walsh also had learned from friends that Thomas had alienated 49ers alumni by throwing out pictures and other relics in a callous bid to remake the team's image. The late Chico Norton, the 49ers equipment manager at the time, rescued many of the items by retrieving them from the trash.

So when Thomas followed up Davis's phone call with one of his own regarding the 49ers coaching position, Walsh told him thanks but no thanks. "He was desperately looking for a coach," Walsh said. "But I would not give any consideration whatsoever to work for Joe Thomas or to leave Stanford at that time. Those were my first contacts about the 49ers job."

While Walsh duplicated a bowl-winning campaign in his second year at Stanford, the 49ers endured another disastrous season in 1978. Pete McCulley was fired after a 1–8 start, and Fred O'Connor went 1–6 the rest of the way.

As the 1978 NFL season neared an end, broadcaster Ron Barr, a mutual friend of Eddie DeBartolo and Walsh, called Walsh to let him know of the 49ers' renewed interest in his candidacy for the coaching job. This time Walsh was prepared

# The Art of the Deal

Talks over the Edward J. DeBartolo family's purchase of the 49ers from the widows of the Morabito brothers were in their final stages in 1977 when the $17.5 million deal nearly fell apart. DeBartolo and his son, Eddie, had flown from Youngstown, Ohio, to Oakland to hammer out the last few details in the Hegenberger Street office of Raiders owner Al Davis, who was brokering the sale. A glitch developed when the elder DeBartolo expressed unhappiness over a last-minute escalation of the price. Some $500,000 had been added to the cost of purchasing a controlling interest in the 49ers from the Morabito family and several limited partners. "I don't do business that way," DeBartolo told Davis. The elder DeBartolo reached for his coat and started to get up to leave.

"Take your coat off and just stay right here. Hear me out," Davis told him. "Take the deal. It's a great deal. And a year from now, you'll double your money."

"Dad, do it. Do it," Eddie DeBartolo said in urging his father to make the purchase. The elder DeBartolo nodded and went from nearly walking away from the purchase to closing the deal in, of all places, Davis's office at the Raiders team headquarters.

"I knew we were going to get a new TV contract and I thought he couldn't go wrong [on buying the 49ers]," Davis said. The value of the team, along with all the other NFL franchises, has skyrocketed since then, multiplying its purchase price many times over.

Among the under-bidders for the purchase of the 49ers was Stockton businessman Alex Spanos. Though that 1977 effort to buy an NFL team didn't work out for him, he would realize his goal seven years later, when he purchased a majority stake in the San Diego Chargers.

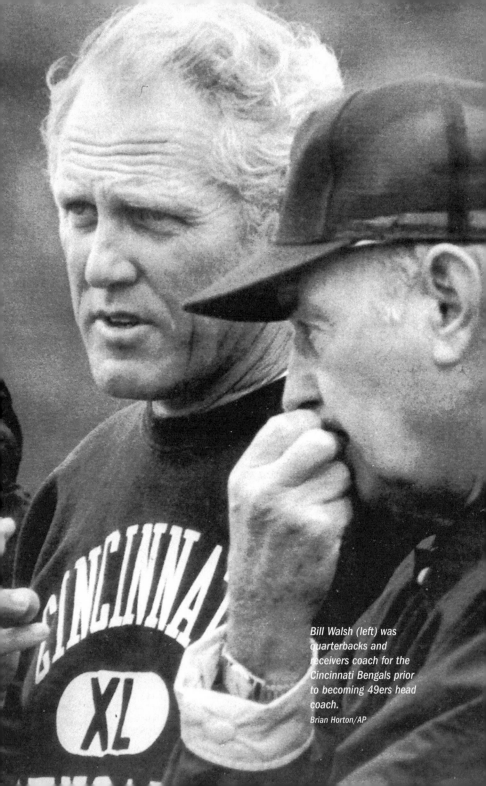

Bill Walsh (left) was quarterbacks and receivers coach for the Cincinnati Bengals prior to becoming 49ers head coach.
Brian Horton/AP

to listen, and the 49ers signaled their readiness to hear him by ousting Thomas, one of the obstacles to his hiring.

A meeting ensued with Eddie DeBartolo, his counsel Carmen Policy, and Walsh at a San Francisco hotel, paving the way for Walsh's hiring. "We just talked and got acquainted," Walsh said. "We had a good conversation. I knew the depth of trouble the 49ers were in, and I could tell him about it more than he could tell me. He had a good feeling about what I wanted to do and I had a good feeling about him because he had ended the turmoil [by firing Thomas]."

DeBartolo liked what he heard from Walsh well enough to give him control over personnel decisions and all other aspects of the football operations. It was unusual for DeBartolo to give that much authority to a first-time NFL head coach, but the initial two years of the family's ownership had been wrenching. So he took what amounted to a leap of faith, and within three years the move he made on gut instinct would be rewarded with the 49ers' first championship. "I had heard through the grapevine that he was an offensive genius," DeBartolo once said. "But it was through my personal interviews with him that I was convinced that he was the man that could bring us all the way."

For Walsh, getting the job was the realization of a long, sometimes frustrating journey toward becoming an NFL head coach. He had spent ten years as an NFL assistant, including eight as the chief offensive strategist under Paul Brown in Cincinnati. That's where he initially thought he would get his chance to ascend to a head-coaching job, but Walsh was passed over when Brown retired. Instead, Brown tabbed defensive coordinator Bill Johnson, a former 49ers center.

# Driving the Bus

It was 1957 and Bill Walsh was looking for his first job as a coach. He found it at Washington High School in Fremont, California, but there was one catch: In addition to the coaching chores, he also had to drive a bus. "When you went to a game, you or one of the guys you worked with had to drive the team to the game," Walsh said. "That was just part of the job, so I learned to drive one of those big school buses."

Walsh inherited a program that had lost twenty-six of its previous twenty-seven games. "I don't think there were others who were interested in the job," Walsh recalled. "I took it for $4,650 a year, including an extra $250 for having a master's degree."

Walsh spent three seasons at the school, turning around a downtrodden program and establishing a pattern of success that foreshadowed his Hall of Fame coaching career and his standing as one of football's great innovators.

Walsh was so distraught by Brown's decision that he left the Bengals in 1976. "I couldn't stay any longer," Walsh said. He became an assistant with the San Diego Chargers and spent a year with Hall of Fame quarterback Dan Fouts, helping him to hone his footwork and overall passing game before joining Stanford for his first major head coaching job. He had coached a semipro team in the mid-1960s in San Jose and also spent three years in the late 1950s as the head coach of Washington High School in Fremont, California.

Bill Walsh took over a team in disarray. "Having been in the league for ten years, I expected an NFL team, and in reality it had been decimated over about a three- or four-year period," Walsh said.

San Francisco's ability to build a team and acquire new talent had been crippled by two major trades that both went sour. In 1976 the 49ers gave New England two number-one picks and quarterback Tom Owen in return for quarterback Jim Plunkett. In 1978 the 49ers sent Buffalo five draft picks, including a number one and two number twos, in exchange for running back O. J. Simpson. Plunkett was cut loose in 1977 after spending two seasons with the 49ers. He would join the Raiders and resurrect his career, winning two Super Bowls. Simpson also played just two seasons before being forced to call it quits after the 1979 campaign, Walsh's first season, because of his aching, arthritic knees.

"There were very few players, a few that turned out to be key, but very few," Walsh said in assessing the pool of talent on the team when he arrived. "I didn't realize until we started playing people, and then it was very evident that we couldn't come close to winning. And I can understand that. I knew the job was almost overwhelming. My good fortune in taking the position is I had authority and responsibility for the entire football operation. So I didn't have to have someone else agree with me. Really, I don't think two people could have done it because they would disagree. It was so intense and there were so many problems.

"Now some great people joined me, some marvelous people including John McVay, Bill McPherson, Bobb McKittrick, Sam Wyche, and others. So we put together a very good coaching staff, but at first, we just couldn't come close with personnel. There were only about half a dozen players I inherited that actually stayed with the team through all of it—Randy Cross,

Bill Walsh and Eddie
DeBartolo Jr. reunite at a
49ers game in 2003.
Paul Sakuma/AP

Fred Quillan, John Ayers, Keith Fahnhorst, Dan Bunz, Willie Harper. So it was very difficult, even overwhelming. But Ed DeBartolo wasn't used to much at that time. He just wanted to see improvement."

That improvement would come in leaps and bounds, beginning with Walsh's first draft in 1979. Despite not having a first-round pick because of the Simpson trade, the 49ers hit the jackpot, laying the foundation for championships to come by using a third-round pick on a spindly legged quarterback named Joe Montana and a tenth-round selection on a tall, lanky wide receiver named Dwight Clark. Then came a refrain. With the 49ers players, they would become words to live by under Bill Walsh: "Line it up. Let's run it one more time."

And one more time after that. And again, and again.

"Bill wanted perfection," said 49ers running back Bill Ring, who played for Walsh from 1981 to 1986. "We'd run a play until we got it exactly right." Walsh was so determined in his pursuit of perfection that sometimes, there literally wasn't enough time in the day to get it done. Ring recalled a 1984 practice marked by Walsh's constant refrains to run the play "one more time." It was starting to get dark, but there was no let up in practice. "Hey man, can you see?" tight end Russ Francis asked teammates in the huddle. Ring and several others answered that they, too, were having trouble making catches in the dark. Francis disappeared from the huddle for a few minutes.

"All of a sudden we see a flashlight staring down at us in the huddle," Ring said. "Everyone looks up, and it's Russ. He had taped a flashlight onto his helmet like a coal miner's lamp. Russ was the one guy on the team who could get away with that

# Looking for a Quarterback

Heading into the 1979 draft, the 49ers had only one quarterback on their roster—Steve DeBerg. So from the time he arrived on the scene in early 1979, head coach Bill Walsh made it a priority to bring in a new quarterback.

Getting recommendations from his scouts, Walsh, along with his quarterbacks coach Sam Wyche, scoured the country in search of the best quarterback prospects. They both worked out Phil Simms and Steve Fuller. Both of them also were on hand for a predraft workout in the Los Angeles area with Notre Dame quarterback Joe Montana. They put Montana through the paces, watching him throw short, medium, and long, and observing his throws on the run and the quickness of his release. "We took about fifteen minutes looking at Joe, and Sam and I said, 'This is the guy,'" Walsh said. "Because his feet were so beautiful, and his athletic ability was so beautiful. He reminded me of Joe Namath in his prime. So he would be our choice."

The selection of Dwight Clark was actually a by-product of the team's quarterback search. Walsh said that while he was at Clemson to work out Fuller, he also decided to take a look at Clark, who was one of Fuller's receivers. "I always liked a big, third-down receiver," Walsh said. "Our scouts said, 'There's a guy at Clemson who's big and can catch the ball.' When we saw him, he really looked the part, and he had good speed as well." And, of course, he became much more than simply a third-down receiver.

Indeed, the selections of Montana in the third round and Clark in the tenth turned out to be among the most fortuitous picks a team ever made. To this day they remain linked in 49ers lore as the beginning and the end of the throw and the catch that changed the course of the team's history.

*Joe Montana was drafted out of Notre Dame in the third round in 1979.* AP

*Walsh, Montana, and DeBartolo Jr. with the Super Bowl XIX trophy in 1985.* AP

because he wasn't intimidated by Bill. We were all laughing." They stopped laughing long enough to run the play, and one more after that, before the bemused Walsh finally gave in and ended practice.

As humorous as the episode appeared, it illustrated the extraordinary attention to detail Walsh demanded from his players, from his coaches, and from himself. "Just the volume of plays we had to know was amazing," Ring said. "Bill's playbook was five times the size of the playbooks I had when I was with the Steelers or in college. Then there were dozens of options for each play, based on our formation and the looks a defense could give us."

While the system was complex, Walsh got to be pretty darn good at teaching the players what he wanted them to know. Tight end Brent Jones, who spent a decade playing for the 49ers, including two years under Walsh, said Walsh made a point of practicing every conceivable situation to give players a frame of reference when they were under fire in a game. The two-minute offense, the four-minute offense to protect a lead late in the game, red-zone plays, goal-line strategy, when to stay in bounds and when not to, when to call time-outs, and who would call time-outs were all parts of the game incorporated into the 49ers' daily practices. "On a daily basis, we worked on the most intricate details of the game in every possible aspect, big and small," Jones said. "And what we practiced on the field we went back over in the classroom."

The scheme brought to San Francisco by the pioneering Walsh came to be known as the West Cost offense. Various offshoots of the system continue to be used widely in the NFL today, including a vestige of the scheme in San Francisco. It was built up and refined in Cincinnati in the early 1970s. Coach Paul Brown and Walsh adapted to the lack of a Bengals running game by designing a timing-based system built on a short, controlled passing game.

"Through a series of formation-changing and timed passes—using all eligible receivers, especially the fullback—we were able to put together an offense and develop it over a period of a time," Walsh said. "In the process, we managed to win our share. The old-line NFL people called it a nickel-and-dime offense. They, in a sense, had disregard and contempt for it, but whenever they played us, they had to deal with it."

For Walsh, installing the system evolved into a science even as its execution on game day was evolving into an art. "The good fortune for me is I installed it, and refitted it, and remolded it in Cincinnati," he said. "Then I installed it in San Diego. A year later, I'm installing it at Stanford, and a couple years after that, I'm installing it with the 49ers. So each year I was able to process that new offense and deliver it to the team and develop it. The changes forced me to be that much more well organized and more specific as to what we taught."

The quarterback was the key to the success of the system, which involved a progression of reads on pass plays designed to get the ball to the open man. "It takes a quarterback who has the working aptitude to play the game and play within a system," Walsh said. "He doesn't necessarily have to have a great arm, but he has to have an accurate arm and a soft touch so the receivers can make the great catches. You can see all the men we've had from Dwight Clark on through—they've been able to make great catches because the ball is thrown softly."

But for all the talk of innovation and impact on the game, Walsh said he was operating on his most basic football instincts when he formulated his version of the West Coast offense. "I've been in a survival mode my entire career," he said, "right up to this day."

# Making the Leap

For 49ers players, the first two years under Bill Walsh were at once uplifting and uncomfortable, dynamic and unsettling. The 49ers were still losing. They went 2–14 for the second straight year in 1979. There was constant roster turnover as part of Walsh's determined, relentless, and, at times, even ruthless search for a winning combination. That included going through forty-two different players over his first two seasons in the secondary alone, Walsh recalled. The revolving door was swinging especially fast in the midst of 1980's eight-game losing streak.

"I saw the tough side of the business," said linebacker Keena Turner, a second-round pick out of Purdue in 1980 who played eleven years for the 49ers. "People kind of came and went. It wasn't very pleasant. I just got the feeling Bill wasn't going to settle for a team that wasn't where he wanted it or a season that wasn't where he thought it should be. I just knew that this guy was going to make changes rapidly if things weren't to his liking."

The sweeping changes and the chronic defeats also weighed on Walsh, who became so emotionally wrung out at times in his second season that he briefly considered quitting. "When you lose fourteen games your first year and eight straight the second, you're thinking, 'How bad can it get?'" said Walsh.

Finally, though, the tide began to turn. The 49ers halted their eight-game skid with back-to-back wins against the New York Giants and New England Patriots. They followed that by pulling out a dramatic 38–35 overtime win against New Orleans, a victory that allowed them to triple the win total from the previous season and latch onto a new feeling of confidence.

The 49ers had overcome a 28-point deficit in what remains the NFL's greatest regular-season comeback. The game also signaled Joe Montana's emergence as the cool, unflappable playmaker at the center of an increasingly dynamic offense, and it marked the 49ers as a team to be reckoned with.

# Tour de Force

There was no stopping Archie Manning and the Saints, or so it seemed to the 49ers, who were trailing 35–7 at halftime on December 7, 1980 at Candlestick Park. Manning had beaten the 49ers' secondary for three long scoring passes, and Jack Holmes had two short touchdown runs around a punt return for a touchdown by Freddie Solomon, the 49ers' lone first-half score. "All I could tell the team at halftime was, 'They figure if it's 35 now, it's going to be 70 by the end,'" Walsh said. "Then I told them, 'If we're going to lose, this is how we're going to lose and it's not going to be by 70. And if we win, here's what we're going to have to do. We'd have to hit 'em. They'd have to fumble.

"And they listened. They had bought into what we were doing and we didn't have any naysayers at all. They were determined to go out and play well in the second half and see what happened. I said we'd have to get some breaks and we did. And it became a tour de force."

Linebacker Keena Turner said he and his teammates didn't need much convincing that they still had a chance to get back in it. "I do remember there was a sense that even though we were down by that much, it wasn't over," Turner said. "I remember Bill saying something to the effect, 'You never know. You get a play here, you get a play there. Just hang in there.' And it happened like he said it would. We got a couple big plays, and all of a sudden it's a game again."

The fabled Joe Montana–Dwight Clark connection came to the fore as part of a comeback that began on the first play of the

# Special Players

**Bill Walsh used every tool at his disposal to build the 49ers into championship contenders, including making trades and picking up other teams' castoffs. Linebacker Jack Reynolds, who would play a big part in an epic goal-line stand in the 49ers' first Super Bowl, was released by the Los Angeles Rams before joining the 49ers in 1981. Defensive end Fred Dean, one of the game's most feared pass rushers, was acquired in a trade a month into the 1981 season after he got into a contract squabble with the San Diego Chargers and their owner, Gene Klein. Tight end Charlie Young, an exceptional blocker and receiver, was picked up in a 1980 trade with the Rams. All three also figured prominently in the 49ers' drive to their first championship. "They were immensely important to us," Walsh said. "They were really competitors, but they were helpful with our young players, too. They were just ideally suited for that team. They gave us chemistry that you rarely see."**

second half. Bottled up at their own 12 yard line, Montana got the 49ers out of the hole by hitting Clark 48 yards downfield. A few plays later, Montana was slicing into the end zone from a yard out.

Just a few minutes after that, Clark gathered in another pass from Montana. He broke in the clear with help from a block from James Owen and completed a 71-yard catch and run for a touchdown, pulling the 49ers to within 35–21 midway through the third quarter. "Their pass coverage, we knew how to break it," Walsh said. "We went in for a couple scores, and the Saints started to question themselves. They started saying 'Oh my God, don't fumble. Don't do anything.' They sort of melted and just were hoping the game would get over, but we kept coming on and did some really great things. And Joe was just outstanding."

The Saints played into the 49ers' hands, committing 3 second-half turnovers, including a fumble that Gerard Williams recovered to set up Montana's 14-yard scoring pass to Solomon. Lenvil Elliott's 7-yard touchdown run with 1:50 left tied it, and safety Dwight Hicks intercepted Manning's last pass of regulation to send the game into overtime. The 49ers won in the extra session on Ray Wersching's field goal to complete a comeback from 28 points down. "That game definitely set a tone, an attitude in us that it's not over, that this team wasn't going to quit," Turner said. "It became part of our heritage for many years after that and something we could draw on in our approach to games."

Walsh said the comeback against the Saints helped to establish a new 49ers identity and distanced the team from its past struggles. "Certainly that was a key game in our development," Walsh said. "We were starting to catch fire as a team. But all that meant to that point was we would be competitive. It didn't mean anything more than that."

Still, the feeling among many players was that there was something magical about the way they came back against New Orleans. The players' confidence in themselves, in each other, and in their coaches was soaring, and together they soon would put the 49ers on a championship course. "Joe Montana came in and did his thing," said Hicks. "Guys after that kind of felt we could win, and the next year we got a couple more players in key positions. From there, we were off and rolling."

*Ronnie Lott celebrates with fans after a
playoff victory in 1981.* Paul Sakuma/AP

# Signature Games, Signature Wins

With one swoop, the 49ers showed how far they had come. With another, they signaled how far they could go. Two games, two wins, both coming in a milestone season.

A year after a crushing 59–14 loss at Dallas, the 49ers turned the tables on "America's Team." John Brodie, who as the 49ers quarterback had lost to the Cowboys three straight years in the playoffs from 1970 to 1972, watched from Candlestick Park's stands as the 49ers took apart his old nemesis 45–14 on October 11, 1981. Wild with joy, Brodie celebrated the victory afterward with a new generation of 49ers just as if it was his own. "When we beat those guys, I've never seen a guy so excited," coach Bill Walsh said. "He was all over the Dallas people. That was the one opponent that we had he just loved to see us beat."

It was the first loss to the 49ers by Dallas coach Tom Landry in five meetings over the previous nine years. "This is something new," Landry mused after the blowout loss. "This is a day for the 49ers to celebrate because it's a great win for them."

Another one was on the horizon. Three weeks later, the 49ers traveled to Pittsburgh to play the Steelers, who were fewer than two years removed from winning their fourth Super Bowl. With Terry Bradshaw and their rugged, physical defense, the Steelers had reigned supreme, beating every NFC team that ventured into Three Rivers Stadium for a decade. But on this day, it would be different, and the 49ers' young secondary of cornerbacks Ronnie Lott and Eric Wright and safeties Carlton Williamson and Dwight Hicks would come of age against the playoff-hardened Steelers.

# A Secondary Comes Together

When the NFC's defensive unit broke the huddle for the January 1985 Pro Bowl at Hawaii's Aloha Stadium, 49ers safety Dwight Hicks took a moment to look around. On either side of him were cornerbacks Ronnie Lott and Eric Wright and safety Carlton Williamson, his secondary teammates with the 49ers.

"You knew it was going to be special from the time we were thrown together, and my assumption turned to reality after the 1984 season, when we were all elected to the Pro Bowl," Hicks said. "Super Bowls are great. That's why we play the game and that's why we compete. But breaking the huddle in Hawaii and seeing the guys I worked with every day, it just doesn't get any better than that. That was special. It hadn't happened before and the way the league is now, I don't know that it will ever happen again."

Nicknamed "Dwight Hicks and the Hot Licks," the 49ers Pro Bowl secondary first came together in 1981 as an experiment born of desperation. Hicks was the lone holdover in a secondary that ranked 27th against the pass in 1980. Determined to tighten the 49ers' pass defense, Walsh dedicated four of the team's five top picks to defensive backs, first drafting Lott out of USC and then Missouri's Wright and Pittsburgh's Williamson. The 49ers also drafted Williamson's Pitt teammate, Lynn Thomas, who played nickel back.

Under secondary coach George Seifert, the 49ers defensive backs molded together to become one of the team's greatest strengths, finishing the 1981 campaign as number-three pass defense in the league.

"There were people saying we were just flailing away, that you can't start rookie DBs in the first place and how can you start, basically, four of them," Walsh recalled. "But my position was every one of the guys we took had been big-time players at big-time programs who had played in big games. Our whole idea was, 'Look, let's just go out and play the game.' We didn't have the problem of some veteran saying, 'Hey, you don't know what you're doing.' Nobody told them that. They just went out and played."

Wright, Hicks, and Williamson each had an interception of Bradshaw, and Lott had a fumble recovery, part of a fierce display that punched holes in the popular image of the 49ers as a finesse team. "I think that's when teams really stood up and took notice of us," said safety Dwight Hicks, a second-year pro playing alongside four rookies that season, including nickel back Lynn Thomas. "We were a team with a mission, a young team, a young secondary that was very motivated. We had players who would hit you, a secondary that forced fumbles and came up with interceptions. That's what made our team so great. Invariably our offense didn't have to go 80 yards to score because we'd be giving them field position."

Williamson hammered that point home with a second-quarter leveling of Steelers wide receiver Calvin Sweeney followed later by a bone-jarring knockdown of John Stallworth.

In the fourth quarter, with the 49ers down 14–10, Williamson swiped an errant Bradshaw pass. That interception, Bradshaw's third of the day, put Joe Montana in position to orchestrate the game-winning drive through the heart of the "Steel Curtain."

In his book, *Building a Champion*, Walsh wrote that the victory in Pittsburgh was among the most exhilarating he and his 49ers teams ever experienced. "We were just jumping up and down and yelling," Walsh wrote. "The excitement was unbelievable."

Linebacker Keena Turner said the 49ers defensive backs carried the day in Pittsburgh, a win that further awakened the 49ers to the notion they were in the midst of something special. "It was the way our secondary played," Turner said. "They were aggressive. They were ferocious. They made plays downfield on a team that was established. The Pittsburgh game and the Dallas game were just monumental for us. Those two organizations were the standard." Beating them helped set the course for the 49ers' unparalleled twenty-year run of success.

## A Championship

Everson Walls was having the game of his life for the Dallas Cowboys and making the mistake-prone 49ers miserable in the 1981 NFC Championship Game at Candlestick Park. The rookie cornerback from Grambling, who led the league with 11 interceptions in the regular season, had an interception and had been all over the field making one tackle after another. When Cowboys linebacker Bob Breunig barreled into fullback Walt Easley and forced a fumble, Walls was right there to recover at midfield, setting up Danny White's go-ahead touchdown pass to tight end Doug Cosbie.

Trailing 27–21 with time running low, the 49ers tried to respond. But Joe Montana's deep, third-down pass for Freddie Solomon was intercepted by the ball-hawking Walls. It was his second swipe of the day and the sixth turnover in the game by the 49ers. "I look back on it now and it probably was the best game I've ever played," Walls said.

If the game had ended at that point, there wouldn't be any question about it. But a defensive stop gave Montana and the 49ers another chance — make that a long-shot chance. The 49ers had the ball at their own 11 yard line with 4:54 remaining. Ninety-one yards and Dallas's confounding flex defense stood between the 49ers and their first trip to the Super Bowl. "In situations like those," Montana said, "I don't fear it. I don't welcome them, but if it's there, I'll take it."

And in the case of the Cowboys' defense, the 49ers took what they gave them right down the field. Dallas believed the 49ers would take to the air because they had to cover so much ground, so the Cowboys lined up in a nickel defense. The alignment, which has an extra defensive back, can be vulnerable to the run. And that wasn't lost on Montana or coach Bill Walsh, who was calling plays from the sideline.

After getting out of the hole with a run and a short completion, Walsh called the first of several power sweeps known as their 18 Bob series, after offensive line coach Bobb McKittrick. Lenvil Elliott, following pulling guards Randy Cross and John Ayers, gained 11 yards with the first one and 7 with the second to put the Cowboys defense on its heels. Then the 49ers crossed the Cowboys up again with an end-around by Freddie Solomon before two completions and another 7-yard sweep by Elliott moved the ball to Dallas's 6 yard line with 58 seconds left. Montana signaled time out and came to the sideline to discuss the third-down play with Walsh.

The call was a Brown left, slot-sprint right option in which Montana would roll out to his right, looking first for Freddie Solomon near the goal line and then Dwight Clark moving along the end line. "It was the natural thing to do, a good solid play that had a very high percentage of completions, anywhere from the 10 yard line to the goal line," Walsh said. "We'd done it many times. It was primarily to Solomon but we had the outlet to Dwight. So Joe was ready—he didn't prefer that, but he was ready to go to Dwight if he had to. But I told him we've got two downs, so let's not force something. But I don't know what the hell I would have called on the fourth down. I was out of answers at that point."

The Cowboys recognized the play and defended it exceptionally well. Solomon was smothered in coverage and Ed "Too Tall" Jones led three charging Dallas defenders who seemed to be just a step away from the furiously backpedaling Montana. "They knew it was coming," Walsh said. "My mistake was not changing the formation somewhat, so that they didn't recognize what was about to happen to them. But they didn't account for Dwight sliding along the end line, and it was just a tremendous play on Joe's part, getting the pass away."

Montana's poise, improvisation, and athleticism—and Clark's fingertips—would rescue the 49ers. Responding to a slight pump fake from Montana, the three defenders all jumped up. When they came back down an instant later, the 49ers quarterback lofted a pass to the back of the end zone for Clark. Walls was right with Clark for the first few seconds of the play but took his eye off him for a split-second to check on Montana. Suddenly, he saw the pass soaring toward him. "Joe was in trouble, and I turned to look back and Dwight had outflanked me," Walls said. "I had drifted too far inside. Dwight was real coy, and he drifted along the back of the end zone toward the left sideline.

"When the ball was on the way, I thought, 'Oh, yeah! It's going to go out of bounds and I'm going to live for another play. He's throwing it out of bounds.' But all of a sudden, you could start to see it die, like it's held up there or something. That's when you see me reaching, knowing it's too late, and Dwight came down with it with a great fingertip catch."

Dallas safety Charlie Waters said after the game that from his end zone vantage point, he could only look on helplessly as

*Dwight Clark snags a key touchdown pass in the 49ers playoff victory over the Dallas Cowboys in 1982.*
Phil Huber/Dallas Morning News/AP

Clark scored the go-ahead touchdown. "He made a spectacular catch. I know because I had a great view," Waters said.

"When I released the ball I knew it was high but I was pretty certain that Clark could get it," Montana told reporters afterward. "It wasn't until I saw the replay that I noticed it was much higher than I thought. D. C. is just a disciplined receiver. He's always where he is supposed to be."

And in this case, it was in midair. "When the ball went up, it was just a matter of me going up and getting it," Clark said. "Joe put it in a place where it either was going to be caught by me or be incomplete. There was no chance of an interception."

There were 51 seconds left when Clark made "The Catch" and Ray Wersching kicked the extra point to put the 49ers on top 28–27. For the Cowboys, "It was bedlam," Walls said. "But my thought process was, 'We got some time left. Please offense, please see if you can score.' I had not given up hope at all."

Wersching's wickedly bouncing kickoff skipped to the Dallas 11 and Timmy Newsome returned it to the Cowboys' 25 yard line. On the first play, Danny White hit Drew Pearson downfield with a pass, and the Cowboys wide receiver came within an eyelash of rendering "The Catch" into an afterthought. Two 49ers defenders collided and Pearson squirted past them. He was starting to run free when Eric Wright stuck his arm out and caught Pearson by the collar, dragging him down one-handed. "Luckily I grabbed him by the back of the shoulder pads," Wright said. "It was a play I had to make."

Dallas's luck ran out after that. Defensive tackle Lawrence Pillers broke through on the subsequent play to sack White, forcing a fumble that Jim Stuckey recovered for the 49ers, who ran out the final few seconds. "That's why Eric collaring Drew Pearson and pulling him down was so memorable as well," Hicks said.

In the end the touchdown-saving tackle by Wright dramatically affected two franchises. It reversed the Cowboys' history of staging dramatic comebacks against the 49ers while preserving the spotlight on Clark's amazing touchdown catch as one of the 49ers' defining moments. "Certainly in defeating Dallas, that play started us on the dynasty," Walsh said. "Now, we had an excellent team. Had we lost that game, we would have learned from it and been back the next year. But it was that play, really, that changed the face of pro football. Yes, it did."

# Quarterback Legacy

The names ring of NFL quarterback royalty: Joe Montana, Steve Young, Frankie Albert, Y. A. Tittle, John Brodie, Jeff Garcia. They had differing styles and differing levels of success, but they did have one common link—all of them were 49ers. Since the 49ers began play in 1946, there has been a nearly unbroken line of stellar play at quarterback. "That's the thing you think about if you've been a fan of the 49ers," said long-

# A Lesson in Quarterbacking

During his Hall of Fame coaching career, Bill Walsh had a well-deserved reputation as one of the game's great quarterback teachers. Consider some of the quarterbacks he tutored: Kenny Anderson, Dan Fouts, Joe Montana, and Steve Young. But before he became a quarterback professor, Walsh was a student. One of his teachers was 49ers quarterback John Brodie, who often visited Walsh while he was an assistant in the early 1960s at Stanford, Brodie's alma mater.

"John would come to the offices at Stanford and he would take the time to talk football with me," Walsh said. "A lot of the mechanics, the footwork, and techniques of the quarterback position, I learned from John. Later I was able to transfer those to many other quarterbacks. But I learned those from John. I didn't have a clue until I talked with John over a period of time."

time football analyst John Madden, who won a Super Bowl as the head coach of the Raiders. "They've had good teams, average teams, and bad teams, but they always seem to have had a good quarterback."

Albert, the first quarterback in the team's history, was ahead of his time, with a scrambling style that foreshadowed the mobile quarterbacks so prevalent in today's NFL. Tittle and Brodie, who followed Albert, were pure passers. Montana, Young, and Garcia combined athleticism and smarts to elevate the 49ers' version of the West Coast offense into one of the most prolific schemes the NFL has seen. "They were throwing the ball all the time but then they had the receivers to catch the passes, from R. C. Owens and Billy Wilson and Clyde Conner right on up to Jerry Rice,"

Madden said. "That's kind of the way the 49ers were built. Sometimes they'd forget to play defense, but they always had that quarterback-receiver thing going."

Even during the last twenty years, marked by some intense and emotional quarterback controversies, free agency, and increased player movement, the 49ers for the most part managed seamless transitions at quarterback. "We have found guys who could move quickly, throw on the run, and were functionally intelligent," said Bill Walsh, who as the 49ers coach or general manager used the draft, a trade, and free agency to bring to the team Montana, Young, and Garcia, in succession. "Joe became one of the two or three greatest quarterbacks in NFL history, with four championships and some incredible performances. We acquired Steve Young, but what was more important was we added a future.

"Steve had a great career of his own. In each case, they weren't marquee players when we got them, and the same with Jeff. What set them apart from other people is their natural instincts for the game and spontaneity in the way they play."

## Frankie Albert: Laying the Foundation

A few days before the team was to conclude its mediocre 1958 season, San Francisco coach Frankie Albert got a phone call summoning him to a meeting with co-owner Vic Morabito at his Hillsborough home. From the timing and tenor of the call, Albert knew his tenure with the 49ers was at an end.

A Stanford All-American who had returned from World War II navy duty to become the 49ers' first quarterback, Albert quietly went through his office at the team's Redwood City practice facility gathering up his precious keepsakes. Then he walked outside and began tossing them to a group of kids whose long-shot hopes for an autograph or two turned into a bonanza of helmets, shoulder pads, jerseys, pictures, plaques, and shoes.

"Gawd, that sight, it tore at me. It still does," said former 49ers broadcaster Bob Fouts, who witnessed the wrenching episode. "He was such a collector, and he had saved that stuff for all those years. They were all things that Frankie treasured. It was just so sad. But I guess he figured this was it and I guess he was done with it, too." Two days after Albert's resignation was disclosed, San Francisco upset the Baltimore Colts 21–12, and Albert walked away a winner in his 49ers' farewell.

That was fitting. After all, Albert won more often than not as a coach and player. But it was his legacy as a leader and swash-buckling playmaker that set him apart even as he set the standard for the 49ers quarterbacks who came after him. "He was the gambler, the greatest gambler in the world on the football field," said Hall of Fame running back Joe Perry, a teammate of Albert's who also played under him as a coach.

"He was a born leader and he did it with such flair," added another 49ers Hall of Famer, Hugh McElhenny. "Frankie more or less ran the club. He had control of the game on game day. Even in practice, if he thought we were working out too much, he'd yell, 'Come on, guys!' And we'd do a circle and go right into the dressing room." More than once 49ers Coach Buck Shaw was left standing there, speechless, while the team followed Albert into the locker room.

Albert played seven years for the 49ers from 1946 to 1952, including the first four years of the team's existence when it estab-lished itself as one of the strongest members of the All-America

Football Conference. The 49ers made the leap to the NFL after the leagues merged prior to the 1950 season.

In today's NFL, the diminutive Albert might never have gotten a chance to play. But the 5'8", 160-pound Albert thrived with the 49ers, relying on his deceptive ball-handling, quickness as a scrambler, and short and medium range passes to good effect. "Frankie was just a spectacular player, a scrambling quarterback, and a great trick player," McElhenny said. "In the old days, the backs would swing out, fake a pitch, there were a lot of fancy plays. And he was a great ball handler."

"He believed in you and himself," Perry added. "First and foremost he believed in himself, and if he believed in you, he knew it was going to work. And nine out of ten times, it worked."

# Y. A. Tittle: The Warrior Quarterback

An opponent once said of Y. A. Tittle that nobody died harder in the pocket than the 49ers quarterback. Nobody pinched harder, either. "Oh, God, was he competitive," said Hall of Fame linebacker Sam Huff, who was both a teammate and an opponent of Tittle. "I remember playing the 49ers at Kezar while I was with the New York Giants. I knocked him down and was lying on top of him and he pinched my stomach as hard as he could. I said, 'Hey! What the hell are you doing?' And he tells me, 'That's what you get for knocking me down!'

"But nobody loved the game more than Y. A. Tittle."

Tittle spent ten years with the 49ers after they made him the number one pick in 1951, and in many ways he was at the forefront of San Francisco's blossoming reputation as a passing team. He had a flair for throwing the deep ball and became a master of

# Off Limits

Y. A. Tittle was one puzzled player during a 1961 preseason game in Portland against the New York Giants. Why, the 49ers quarterback wondered, were some of the Giants' fiercest defensive players exhibiting such tender behavior toward him?

One time, recalled Tittle, their star defensive end, Andy Robustelli, broke through and had the 49ers quarterback in his sights. At the last instant, he veered away from a direct hit in favor of shoving Tittle—gently—to the ground. "Then he picked me up, brushed me off, and asked if I was okay," Tittle said. "Here they had guys like Sam Huff, Jim Katcavage, Rosey Grier, and Robustelli, and I wasn't getting much of a pass rush at all. I just sat back there and picked 'em apart. It was the easiest game I'd ever played in my life."

It wasn't until afterward that Tittle found out why. Huff caught up with him after the game as he walked off the field. "He says, 'Congratulations, you're a Giant,'" Tittle remembers. The trade in which the Giants would send guard Lou Cordileone to the 49ers in return for Tittle had been agreed to in the hours before the exhibition, but it wasn't formally consummated until later. "My owner, Wellington Mara, tells us, 'Don't hit Y. A. Tittle, don't hurt him, because he belongs to the Giants,'" Huff said. "If you do, it's a $1,000 fine. Well, cripes, how are you going to play a game without hitting the quarterback? He had all night to throw the ball."

the screen play, using strong, elusive runners such as Hugh McElhenny, Joe Perry, and J. D. Smith to take the short pass and move downfield.

The rapport he developed with game-breaking receivers such as Clyde Conner, Gordy Soltau, Billy Wilson, and R. C. Owens, with whom he executed the famed "Alley-Oop," also took the 49ers' passing game to new heights. "He was just terrific, the most accurate passer I played with in pro football," McElhenny said. "Yeah, he'd throw some interceptions. His wife used to say to my wife up in the stands, 'I think he's colorblind sometimes.' But he was a tough competitor. In the huddle, he took total control and backed down to nobody. And he knew football, he understood football."

There were times when Tittle's sheer competitiveness got the better of him, never more so than in the bitter cold of Chicago in 1963. Tittle, who joined the Giants in a trade before the 1961 season, had led them to a third straight appearance in the NFL championship. After losing both of their previous title matches to the Green Bay Packers, the Giants were clinging to a 10–7 halftime lead over the Bears. But Tittle had wrenched his knee badly on a second quarter hit. "They're inside at halftime taping him up to go back out there," Huff said. "We're beating them, and I know we have the defense that can hold 'em. I say, 'Y. A., don't play this half. Don't do it. We've got 'em. You'll wear the ring.' But they fix him up. He plays the second half and throws another interception. They score a touchdown, the only other one that they get, and beat us 14–10."

Tittle played only one more season, but it was long enough to leave the game with one of its most searing portraits. Morris Berman of the *Pittsburgh Post-Gazette* took the famous picture of the bent, dazed, and bloodied Tittle in the aftermath of the devastating end zone hit by Steelers defensive lineman John Baker in a September 1964 game. Baker caught Tittle square in the chest and drove him to the ground, the impact knocking off Tittle's helmet. The force of the blow also tore the cartilage in his sternum and blood could be seen trickling down the side of his face from a cut near his ear.

## John Brodie: A Defining Drive

It happened in a flash five weeks into the 1972 season. New York Giants defensive tackle Jack Gregory barreled into John Brodie just as the 49ers quarterback was about to throw. Brodie's left foot got stuck in the turf, and the quarterback fell to the ground and twisted his ankle sharply. The pain was searing and intense, and for the only time in his seventeen-year career, Brodie was put on a stretcher and carried off the field.

Steve Spurrier took over at quarterback and got the 49ers back on track, winning five, with one tie, in an eight-game span. That put the 49ers in position to clinch their third straight NFC West title with a win over the Minnesota Vikings in the season finale.

Brodie had dressed for the Rams' game the previous week, but coach Dick Nolan had stuck with Spurrier. The Minnesota game began the same way, with Brodie on the bench. But as the fourth quarter approached and the 49ers trailed 17–6, Nolan talked over a quarterback change with Jim Shofner, the receivers and quarterbacks coach. "It's not going very well, and Dick says to me, 'I want Brodie to go in,'" Shofner said. "Dick just felt we needed something different."

The switch to Brodie, playing for the first time in two months, didn't look good initially. The first two passes he threw were intercepted, and the next time he got the ball, it was at the 49ers' own 1 yard line. "The first play, he gets us out of the hole by hitting Ted Kwalick for about 30 yards up the seam," Shofner said. "That impressed me."

Brodie, who called his own plays, took the 49ers on a 99-yard touchdown drive, pulling the 49ers to within 17–13. With 90 seconds left, the 49ers got the ball back at their 34. It took Brodie one minute to move the 49ers to another touchdown, which came when Dick Witcher out-jumped Charlie West in the corner of the end zone to haul in the quarterback's game-winning pass. "Whenever I think of John, that's the game I think of," Shofner said.

What happened immediately after the victory stuck with Brodie—who had been taunted and booed many times—for a lifetime. Fans jumped over Candlestick Park's railings and swarmed onto the field, seeking out Brodie and lifting him up on their shoulders. They carried him off the field in a frenzied—and overdue—tribute before setting him down in front of the players' locker room entrance.

Brodie played one more season before retiring, but it is the year-end victory and the impromptu celebration that followed that stand out as a final triumph in a brilliant, tumultuous career. "He carried the team through some of the roughest times and some of the best times," Bill Walsh said. "But beyond that, what he could do, you don't see much now in football. He had touch on his passes. He could throw the soft screen pass or he could throw the ball over someone's head. He could drill the ball if he needed to. He was an absolute technician and an artist, one of the great performers at the quarterback position in history."

Tackle Len Rohde said that as well as Brodie knew the game, it was his ability to bring out the best in his teammates that stood out as the true measure of his greatness at quarterback. "When he could connect with somebody, he would tell us, 'Give me just a little extra time and I can get six,'" Rohde said. "When he said that, he usually meant it, and it gave us a lot of confidence that if we really busted our butts, he'd make it happen. And I'd say more often than not, he did."

## Joe Montana: The 49ers' Confidence Man

When Joe Montana joined the 49ers in 1979, his initial duties were to back up quarterback Steve DeBerg and serve as place-kicker Ray Wersching's holder. "He was so good," Wersching said. "It didn't matter where the ball was snapped. He'd always put it down in the right spot for me. He made my job so much easier."

As a favor to Wersching, Montana kept holding for him even after he became the 49ers full-time starter in 1981. "Every year at training camp, I'd say, 'Come on, Joe, hold for me, please?'" Wersching said. "And he'd say, 'Oh, all right.' He held for me for a lot of years." Montana didn't stop holding for Wersching until 1986, after returning from a serious back injury. But Wersching said that in many ways he owes his record of consistency and reliability over his eleven-year career with the 49ers to Montana.

"In the huddle, Joe was always right next to me, so I'd always just put my hand on his shoulder and pat it," Wersching said. "It was like a little sense of security. The thing was, for all of us, whenever Joe stepped on the field, he generated an air of confidence. We all had seen him come through so many times before, so just having him out there boosted our confidence, too. It was like, 'Oh, yeah, we can do this.'"

# The Price of Controversy

The trade rocked the 49ers with the force of an emotional earthquake. Imagine shipping away Joe Montana, whose savvy and clutch play under pressure was the center of the team's first four Super Bowl titles, to Kansas City in exchange for a number one draft pick. That's what happened before the 1993 season.

With Montana healthy again after missing all or parts of the last two seasons with elbow problems, the 49ers had to determine whether to return the job to him, throw it open to a competition, or allow Young to remain in place. Coach George Seifert's inclination was to keep Steve Young in place. After four years as Montana's backup, Young had taken hold of the job with stellar play, winning the first of his two league MVP awards while Montana was sidelined. Montana believed it was unfair to lose his starting job because of injury.

With the long-running controversy between Montana and Steve Young threatening to create divisions on the team, the 49ers knew they had to come to some sort of resolution. Team brass decided Montana had to go, though at the last moment, club owner Eddie DeBartolo, who remained loyal to Montana, tried to work out a compromise that would have kept both quarterbacks in San Francisco.

It was Montana who finally put a stop to the melodrama, telling DeBartolo and team president Carmen Policy that he'd rather move on and play elsewhere than ride the bench in San Francisco. "In retrospect, it was the right thing for everybody, and Joe was the greatest realist of all," Policy said after the trade. "It would have been very difficult, almost impossible, with both of them here."

Joe Montana set the standard for
49ers quarterbacks. *Joe Robbins*

Montana instilled that anything-is-possible belief in his teammates time and again in his fourteen years with the 49ers. They had seen him put together the drive ending in Dwight Clark's game-winning touchdown catch in the 1981 NFC title game and the pressure-packed march culminating with a scoring pass to John Taylor with just seconds to spare in Super Bowl XXIII following the 1988 season.

Fullback Tom Rathman remembers a comeback victory against the powerful Philadelphia Eagles in 1989 as emblematic of Montana's ability to rally his teammates in the face of incredible adversity. Montana had been battered by a ferocious Eagles pass rush that had broken through for 8 sacks. Reggie White, Clyde Simmons, and Mike Pitts seemed to be taking turns knocking Montana down. "They were bringing the heat, man," Rathman said. "Buddy Ryan had the Navajo front going to put pressure on Joe. But they were also blitzing and vacating the middle, and we knew that if we could protect and just give Joe some time, we were going to burn them."

For three quarters, the Eagles were winning. But Montana and the 49ers owned the fourth period. That was when Montana threw 4 of his 5 touchdown passes, connecting with John Taylor, Jerry Rice, Brent Jones, and Rathman to twice overcome 11-point deficits for a 38–28 win. "I think we've all seen it written that Joe is the finest comeback quarterback in the game," 49ers coach George Seifert said after witnessing the furious fourth. "His cool under pressure is unbelievable. His ribs were taped up, he was hurting, but he still got the job done."

Even Ryan, who was doing everything he could to get in Montana's face that day, had to tip his hat to the 49ers quarterback. "Normally when you score 28 points you should win, but not when you're up against a guy like Montana," Ryan said.

Rathman could have easily told him that. "I think when you talk about playing football, as a quarterback, I'd say probably 60 to 75 percent of the plays work the way they're designed to," Rathman said. "But the other percentage, you've got to get your quarterback to create something. That's the thing Joe could do. He not only could drop back and work out of the pocket, with all the timing and precision that required, but he also could get the scramble drill going, buying himself time and getting outside of the pocket to look for a window to throw the football through. I think he really defined what the quarterback is for the West Coast offense."

## Steve Young: Passing on the Run

It was the day after a desperate, backpedaling Steve Young threw a 25-yard touchdown pass to Terrell Owens to beat the Green Bay Packers in a January 1999 wild-card playoff game with 3 seconds remaining. As Young and the other 49ers offensive players gathered for a team meeting at the club's Santa Clara facility, offensive line coach Bobb McKittrick jotted the number 4,400 on a display board. "I told them, 'This is how many passes he has thrown here, and I've seen every one of them, and there's none that was as great a pass as that one," McKittrick said.

McKittrick's observation illustrated just how far Young had come since Bill Walsh pulled off the 1987 trade with Tampa Bay that brought Young to San Francisco. A swift, elusive runner, Young was viewed at the time as a one-dimensional quarterback prone to forsaking the pass and taking off downfield, sometimes desperately, to try to move the ball on his own. The results had been awful in his two seasons with Tampa Bay as well as his two seasons in the United States Football League.

But where others saw a hopeless, undisciplined scrambler, Walsh saw the potential for melding Young's throwing ability with his brilliance as a runner. "When he came here, Steve was pretty shaken up related to his self-confidence and shaken up as to what he might accomplish on the football field," Walsh said. "Really, Steve had spent a number of seasons just being totally frustrated and maligned. By the time we got him, he was extremely anxious to be part of this organization because this was really his last chance to become a viable NFL player. Down the road, there was some greatness, but at the time he really didn't have a grasp of the offense."

Initially, the 49ers had to wrestle with the two sides of Young, which could take turns surfacing from one play to the next. A 1988 game against Minnesota exemplified the dichotomy. Young, starting in place of injured Joe Montana, threw a 73-yard touchdown pass to John Taylor and then won the game in the last two minutes. He put together a twisting, tackle-breaking 49-yard run, staggering the final few yards into the end zone to complete a daunting trek seemingly through the entire Vikings defense. Walsh continues to regard Young's run as one of the greatest individual efforts he's seen on the field of play, but it also reinforced the notion that he needed more schooling and coaching to work within the system. "It was up to us to sort of tie a stake to him and keep him in the pocket," Walsh said.

Young had to bide his time to become the complete quarterback, spending his first four seasons with the 49ers as Montana's backup. But he learned from watching Montana

# Unforgettable

The play came in as a "3-Jet All Go," which calls for the receivers to streak downfield. As Steve Young pulled back from center, he tripped over a loose clump of turf and nearly went down. But he regained his footing, spotted Terrell Owens in the middle of the field, and threaded the pass to him among three defenders.

Owens made a tremendous catch, holding onto the ball after being leveled by near simultaneous body blows in the end zone from Darren Sharper and Pat Terrell. The 25-yard scoring pass with 3 seconds left lifted the 49ers past the Green Bay Packers 30–27 in a wild-card playoff game at Candlestick Park on January 3, 1999. "I had to throw it a little bit to the right, so he got a 'Hello' from one safety and a 'Good luck' from the other," Young said. Owens answered with a determined "Hang on" even as he got flattened in the end zone.

"You know, they were only rushing three guys and I was uncovered, so I had one of the best seats in the house," guard Ray Brown said. "It was an unbelievable throw and catch. I just threw my hands up and started crying. It was one of the best feelings I'd ever experienced."

Both the throw and the catch, which helped end a three-year losing streak to the Packers in the playoffs, drew comparisons to the fabled Montana-Clark connection in the 1981 NFC Championship Game. "That play will be attached to 49ers lore for a long time. I'll always remember it," Young said.

*Terrell Owens makes his amazing reception against the Packers in their 1999 playoff game.* Susan Ragan/AP and, after Walsh's departure in 1989, benefited from the offensive coaching of Mike Holmgren, Mike Shanahan, and Gary Kubiak.

In 1994 Young joined Montana as the only other 49ers quarterback to lead the team to a Super Bowl title, punctuating the team's 49–26 victory over San Diego by throwing for 6 touchdowns. On the way to the 49ers' fifth championship, Young had become one of the NFL's premier passers, at one point winning four straight league passing titles and becoming the first 4,000-yard passer in team history.

Two weeks earlier, as Young celebrated the 49ers' 1994 NFC championship victory over Dallas with a frenetic, hand-waving dash around Candlestick Park, former 49ers public relations man Rodney Knox couldn't help thinking that Young, the running quarterback, had come full circle. "There were times at the end of games, when he was backing up Joe, that he would actually run around the field, take laps, just to release some energy," Knox said. "Then to see him on that victory lap—man, I just thought, 'He used to do this out of frustration. Now, he is doing it as a starting quarterback out of pure joy.' It was unforgettable."

# Jeff Garcia: In the Shadow of Legends

Jeff Garcia was in the midst of a disheartening run. The quarterback from nearby Gilroy who grew up watching Joe Montana and Steve Young play for San Francisco had been benched in the middle of the 1999 season after a string of ineffective outings.

Garcia had won his first NFL start, helping the 49ers beat Tennessee a week after Steve Young suffered a career-ending concussion at Arizona. But his play went downhill after that, culminating in a miserable 7-for-18 passing performance for 39 yards in a loss to Pittsburgh that led coach Steve Mariucci to sit him down. "We had brought Jeff in to be a veteran backup," offensive coordinator Greg Knapp said of Garcia, a San Jose State product who starred in the Canadian Football League for five years before signing on with the 49ers. "Then when Steve was injured, Jeff was thrown in there, obviously sooner than we anticipated. It was hard on him because he was learning on the run."

While Garcia sat out the next three games in favor of Steve Stenstrom, Knapp put together what in essence was a highlight film of Garcia's fifty best plays. "It covered the things he had done in the preseason and during the regular season, all of them positive plays," Knapp said. "Then we sat him down and told him, 'Look, you've shown me and you've shown the coaches you can do this, and here's the proof.' I think he took that and ran with it. It carried over to his next game and got his confidence going again, which is so vital, especially for a quarterback." Said Garcia, "It showed me I could play this game."

Then he proceeded to show everyone else. Despite a 44–30 loss at Cincinnati in miserable weather conditions, Garcia passed for 437 yards and 3 touchdowns in a startling return to the lineup. "It definitely was a kick-start to get me headed back in the right direction," Garcia said. "When I came back after sitting for those games, I just had a new awareness, a new outlook. It was like, I'm going to get back to having fun. I'm going to get back to enjoying myself and take the pressure off and just go out there and let it fly. I started to give the guys around me opportunities to make plays, and they were coming through."

He endured another setback or two, but fended them off to establish himself as a worthy successor to the 49ers' storied quar-

Jeff Garcia stepped into
some big shoes when he
became the 49ers
starting quarterback.
*Joe Robbins*

# Garcia, Off the Cuff

**Back in 1992 while he was still playing quarterback at San Jose State, Jeff Garcia ran into one of his heroes in a downtown San Jose nightclub: Jerry Rice, who happened to be sitting by himself listening to music. Garcia decided to go up and introduce himself to the 49ers star, already widely regarded as the greatest receiver the NFL had ever known. "I said, 'Hey, one day I'm going to be throwing passes to you,'" Garcia recalled with a laugh. "I don't know. I probably was a little overconfident or feeling good about myself. I'm sure it wasn't the first time he heard something like that. But for me, it was something that I always remembered."**

**And something he made come true seven years later, when he joined the 49ers in 1999 as a free agent after starring in the Canadian Football League for five years.**

terback legacy. "Here's a guy who had to fill the shoes of two of the greatest quarterbacks in NFL history, Hall of Famers," Knapp said. "All he does is go to the Pro Bowl three years in a row, without the same kind of supporting cast that they had. When the 49ers were going through salary cap hell the first time, Jeff was just tearing it up, and he tore it up against defenses that knew we had to throw because we were so often behind."

Garcia went on to lead the 49ers to the playoffs twice in his four years as their starter. "The thing about Jeff Garcia is he's a gamer," said former Raiders coach and longtime football analyst John Madden. "I mean, you watch him throw the ball in practice and he has to put everything he has into it. Even when he's playing catch, you wouldn't say he's a strong-armed guy. But then you look at him in a game and you say, 'Shoot, he's one of the best.'"

# Trial and Triumph

Offensive lineman Jesse Sapolu remembers it as one of the most beautiful passes he's ever seen. Freddie Solomon reached out and caught the 76-yard touchdown pass from Joe Montana without breaking stride. It was the middle score in a 21-point fourth-quarter surge that pulled the 49ers even with the Washington Redskins in the NFC Championship Game at RFK Stadium on January 7, 1984. "It was just an unbelievable strike by Joe," said Sapolu, a rookie 49ers lineman that season. "I've seen a lot of players that had stronger arms, but you talk about someone throwing one strike after another, that's Joe."

After a disappointing and divisive 3–6 campaign during the strike-shortened 1982 season, the 49ers reclaimed the NFC West crown to return to the playoffs. They seemed on the verge of another trip to the Super Bowl. Their fourth-quarter scoring spree—Montana threw two touchdown passes to Mike Wilson around the long bomb to Solomon—took fewer than three minutes. To this day, Bill Walsh says Montana may never have played so well and done so much in so little time in a game.

The 49ers' rally had left what had been a raucous sold-out crowd at RFK Stadium in stunned silence, but it ultimately would be for naught. Taking over with some seven minutes left, the Redskins drove 78 yards to a field goal, aided by two penalty calls on cornerbacks Eric Wright and Ronnie Lott that the 49ers, then and now, view with disdain. "No question we got jobbed," Walsh said. "There wasn't anything there to call. The ball went 10 yards over their heads both times. They were not catchable. I mean, it was just bizarre."

Washington, facing a second-and-10 from its 45, sent Art Monk against Wright on a sideline pattern. Wright put his left hand on Monk's back, which drew a pass interference penalty after officials ruled the ball was indeed catchable. The penalty gave the Redskins a first down at the 49ers' 18 yard line. Moments later, on a third-and-5 play, Lott was jamming Charlie Brown off the line of scrimmage and was called for holding him, giving the Redskins a first down. Mark Moseley came on to kick the game-winning 25-yard field goal with 44 seconds left. "It was going to be our game, but it didn't turn out that way because of those calls," Sapolu said.

But 1983, including the final bitter loss, nevertheless proved to be the seminal season in the run-up to the 49ers dynasty. The team quietly resolved to do what it could to keep games out of officials' hands, and the 49ers' return to the playoffs filled them with a new confidence that they could get back to the postseason again and again. "The strike season in 1982 was such a negative year mentally, for the coaching staff and the team as well," Sapolu said. "And the thought was there by some people that maybe what the 49ers did in 1981 was a fluke. What we did in 1983 was reestablish the 49ers as one of the elite teams, and we built from there. We started to set the standard of making the playoffs every year. There were times we didn't go all the way, but the realization around the league was the 49ers are there and they're going to be there again."

Walsh agreed that even though the 49ers fell short, the 1983 campaign was pivotal. It paved the way for a magnificent 1984 season in which the 49ers lost just one game, set a franchise record for wins in a season, and rolled to their second Super Bowl title. "That Washington game was a springboard, just as that '83 season was a springboard," Walsh said. "When we came back to start again the next year, we had tremendous confidence. We had put together, really, a fine team. We added some players, and we felt confident all the way through."

By 1987 the 49ers had coalesced into a juggernaut. That year the squad finished the season with the league's top-ranked defense and the top-ranked offense. Jerry Rice was coming to the fore as the league's top receiver, complemented by the fleet, rugged John Taylor. The 49ers had both Joe Montana and Steve

# Quality Depth

One of the keys to the 49ers' great success in 1984 was the team's depth on both sides of the ball. A year after getting running back Wendell Tyler and tight end Russ Francis in separate trades, Bill Walsh made a series of moves prior to the 1984 season to shore up the defensive side of the ball.

In deals with San Diego, the 49ers acquired veteran defensive linemen Louie Kelcher and Gary "Big Hands" Johnson. They also completed a trade with Seattle to bring defensive tackle Manu Tuiasosopo. The acquisition of the thirty-something defensive linemen and the drafting of Michael Carter left the 49ers with a dominating defensive line. "We were like eight deep on the defensive line," Walsh said. "All the backup linemen were Pro Bowl players. They were all older players nearing the end of their careers, and we were able to acquire them because they wanted to play for us. But when we'd go deep into a game and they would rotate in, they would be just as good as our starters. They were part of a really good football team all the way through. It has to be one of the best teams of all time."

Young on the roster, and Roger Craig and Tom Rathman were brought together to form a dynamic backfield. They stormed to a 13–2 record. "That team was totally dominating," said Sapolu.

The oddsmakers gave the Minnesota Vikings virtually no chance to beat the mighty 49ers, who were in the postseason for a fifth straight year, in the divisional playoffs. But the 49ers failed to handle the Vikings pass rush anchored by Chris Doleman and Keith Millard, and the 49ers secondary had no answer for the acrobatic catches—10 of them—by Anthony Carter. "They had already projected us winning the Super Bowl by 3 touchdowns, and we had one bad game," Bill Walsh said. Sapolu had this to say: "We were out of sync. Minnesota just got us at the right time."

Center Randy Cross said the loss still rankles him. "It was a combination of Anthony Carter having a career day and us coming in a little overconfident," Cross said. "We had such a good team, and to lose like that is something that still gnaws at me."

The ramifications from the shocking upset were deep and lasting. The 49ers' longest-running quarterback controversy took root when Walsh benched an ineffective, but healthy, Montana, already a two-time Super Bowl winner, in the third quarter in favor of Young. "If I was just a person on the sideline, I wouldn't have done it, but as a coach, I had to make the change," Walsh said. "It had slipped away from us and Steve represented the only chance, with his running, to get the ball off because their pass rush was killing us. And Steve's running did help. He made some big runs, accounted for a couple touchdowns, but we didn't come close."

Owner Eddie DeBartolo, who lavished his players with perks and some of the highest salaries in the league—and had come to expect championships in return—took the loss especially hard. Walsh bore the brunt of that unhappiness, though he maintains there was never a cross word between them during the episode. "I don't know if ticked off is the word—he was furious," Walsh said. "But it wasn't the players. He didn't blame the players. It was me. That was a traumatic experience, so there was some upheaval in the organization."

DeBartolo considered firing Walsh but settled for stripping him of his title as team president and installing himself as the club's chief executive. Walsh said he believes that Carmen Policy, DeBartolo's attorney and later the 49ers' team president, helped persuade DeBartolo to retain him. "What I do know is I couldn't leave on that note, though I'm not sure Eddie didn't want me to," Walsh said. "I think Carmen helped me there because who knows what would have happened if Carmen hadn't intervened?"

The 49ers rallied the following season to win the championship, but it didn't come easily. Back-to-back losses in Arizona and to the Raiders dropped the 49ers to 6–5 and set off an intense round of internal questioning. "We had just blown a 23-point fourth-quarter lead in Arizona and then the Raiders came to Candlestick Park and shut us down," said Sapolu. "None of us was taking it too well."

That included owner Eddie DeBartolo, who met with Walsh after the 49ers' 9–3 loss to the Raiders. Walsh was wrung out and unsure whether he had the stamina emotionally to keep coaching. He and DeBartolo decided to wait to make a final decision on his future until after the season, though Walsh was leaning toward leaving. "There were just some times where it looked as though there was no reason to keep going through this, no reason to have to live like this," Walsh said of the pressing weight to win. "Eddie and I had a good, long conversation about everything. We discussed all the options. We ended up deciding to decide what we were going to do after the year was over. I don't know, I probably felt freed of worry about what was going to happen. I just wasn't going to worry about it anymore."

DeBartolo and Walsh were not the only distressed parties to meet in the aftermath of the loss to the Raiders, one of the few times the 49ers had failed to score a touchdown in a game since

Walsh had arrived in 1979. "We had a players-only meeting the day after that game," Sapolu said. "Nobody thought we were any good any more, but guys in that room thought different. We knew we were the best team in the league if we got on track because we basically had the same players from a year earlier." That was when the 49ers led the league in most significant offensive and defensive categories.

"I really think that meeting started something special," Sapolu said. "We just stood up and said, 'Hey, it's time to establish ourselves as a Super Bowl team.' And we could do it because we still controlled our own destiny. We just had incredible focus."

Center Randy Cross said it was one of the few times he remembers a players-only meeting actually working. "Most of the time you discount their importance, but this one really did something besides giving us a platform to air the issues," Cross said. "There were so many critics, inside the team and out, but the general consensus we came away with was that we could win in spite of any problems that we had, and that's what we did."

Fullback Tom Rathman concurred. "As players," he said, "we didn't need a lot of motivation. We knew we were good enough to do it, and then we became the hottest team in the league."

The 49ers did indeed go on a four-game tear, clinching the NFC West title. After losing a meaningless regular-season finale to the Los Angeles Rams, they rolled through the postseason, starting by dispatching the Minnesota Vikings 34–9 to gain a measure of revenge for their wrenching playoff defeat a year earlier. The following week, on a cold, bitter day in Chicago where the wind chill reached 26 degress below zero, the 49ers dominated the Bears 28–3 in the NFC Championship Game. "So many people were saying we were going to have a tough time in the cold weather, and in reality we had no problem in it," said Rathman.

From the outset, the 49ers took advantage of the Bears' propensity to blitz. Jerry Rice went deep and Rathman picked up blitzing middle linebacker Mike Singletary, helping to give Joe Montana time to connect downfield with Rice for a 61-yard touchdown strike in the first quarter. "We hit a home run on that play," Rathman said. "And we kept having success running and passing. Everything just jelled." And carried the 49ers on to another Super Bowl.

Near the end of the 1988 season, Walsh had confided to DeBartolo that he planned to resign. But after the team put together its improbable Super Bowl run, DeBartolo and team executive Carmen Policy called a meeting with Walsh in Carmel to try to persuade him to remain. "They wanted me to stay and coach, and offered me more money, but I said, 'No, I think I should step away,'" Walsh said.

Walsh said he would stay on as general manager and recommended that DeBartolo hire his top assistant, defensive coordinator George Seifert, to take over as the 49ers coach. With uncertainty swirling around the 49ers hierarchy, Seifert had left to interview for the Cleveland Browns head coaching job. But during a layover, he called his wife, who told him the 49ers had called and wanted him to come back to talk about becoming their coach. Seifert canceled the interview in Cleveland and headed back home to succeed Walsh.

Walsh only stayed a few more months as general manager before leaving the 49ers entirely to become an analyst for NBC Sports. He now considers the three-year move to television as "probably the dumbest thing I've ever done. Oh, geez, getting into that and being on the road for twenty-three straight weekends a

# Regrets? He Has a Few

Bill Walsh had won three Super Bowls in ten years as the 49ers coach and general manager when he walked away from the organization in early 1989. Sometimes he wishes he didn't. "I left them with the youngest team and the best team in football," Walsh said. "They were champions. They had the attitude. They had all the offense together. I just walked away from something like that, which wasn't very smart. Gosh, I easily could have been involved in a couple more Super Bowl wins. But that's how it ended."

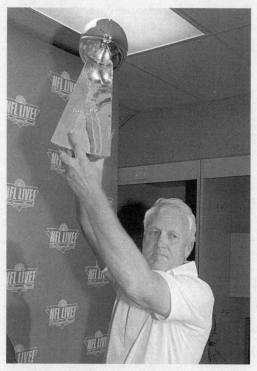

*Bill Walsh raises the trophy after the 49ers won Super Bowl XXIII in 1989.*   Ed Reinke/AP

year, there wasn't any real gratification doing it, and for me, it just wasn't what I wanted to be," Walsh said. "I missed football and I should have been in football, even if I'd gone to another team."

Walsh would return to football, rejoining Stanford for a second tour as coach in 1992 after some initial feelers to come back to the 49ers in some capacity were rebuffed. He eventually made his first return to the 49ers in 1996 as an offensive consultant under Seifert. Later he would come back as the 49ers general manager to help shepherd the organization through an ownership squabble, salary cap problems, and a rebuilding of the team into a contender.

Despite the loss of Walsh, these were heady days for the 49ers. Under first-year coach George Seifert, they blew out Denver to claim their second straight Super Bowl title (game XXIV) in January of 1990. That made them the first team to win back-to-back championships since the Pittsburgh Steelers did it in Super Bowls XIII and XIV.

In the flush of their 55–10 victory over the Broncos, the 49ers set an even loftier goal. "We got the repeat," a giddy Roger Craig chanted. "Now we want the three-peat."

No team had ever won three Super Bowls in a row, and the 49ers wanted to be the first. They would come awfully close.

The 49ers finished the 1990 season with a 14–2 record and entered the NFC playoffs as the number one seed. They rolled past the Washington Redskins 28–10 in the divisional playoffs, setting up a meeting with the Bill Parcells–coached New York Giants in the NFC Championship Game at Candlestick Park on January 20, 1991.

The Giants defense gave ground grudgingly. The 49ers defenders were every bit as unyielding. First-half scoring was limited to two field goals apiece by the 49ers' Mike Cofer and the Giants' Matt Bahr. In the third quarter the 49ers broke through for the game's only touchdown when Joe Montana connected with John Taylor on a 61-yard touchdown pass. But the Giants' relentless pass rush eventually would doom Montana. "We hit Montana clean and hard, again and again," Lawrence Taylor, the Giants' great pass-rushing linebacker, told reporters afterward.

The last hit was the worst, not only finishing Montana's day but, for all practical purposes, his career with the 49ers. With just over nine minutes remaining and the 49ers leading 13–9, Leonard Marshall leveled Montana with a blindside hit to his back just as he was getting ready to throw. Initially Marshall had been toppled by a body block from fullback Tom Rathman, but the burly defensive end scrambled to his feet and dashed 15 yards across the field, barreling into Montana from behind. Montana was knocked to the ground with such force that he broke his right hand and bruised his chest.

Steve Young came off the bench to finish the game, which would be Montana's last meaningful appearance in a 49ers uniform. His hand injury healed but elbow problems surfaced that sidelined him for virtually all of the next two years, and he was traded to Kansas City before the 1993 season.

Bahr kicked his fourth field goal, pulling the Giants to within 13–12, after the Giants executed a fake punt midway through the fourth quarter that caught the 49ers with only ten men on the field. An instant before the ball was hiked on the fourth-and-2 play from the Giants' 46 yard line, return man John Taylor noticed the 49ers were short, but by then it was too late to signal a time-out. Linebacker Bill Romanowski had been

injured on the play preceding the punt, and his replacement didn't get on the field in time, according to Seifert.

"I just thought, 'Damn, somebody is missing,'" Taylor said. "I couldn't get a time-out called. It was like a 'What-are-we-going-to-do-now-type deal.' Then they ran the play right up the right side where the man was supposed to be." Gary Reasons, the Giants' upback on the punt team, took a direct snap from center and shot through a hole that opened up off tackle. He rumbled 30 yards to the 49ers' 24 yard line before finally being stopped.

Still, the 49ers had a 1-point lead and the ball and needed only a few more first downs to secure their third straight trip to the Super Bowl. Steve Young hit tight end Brent Jones down the middle for a 25-yard gain, and two runs by Roger Craig produced another first down at the Giants' 40 yard line. "We had it right there. We had the game won," 49ers linebacker Matt Millen said.

Not quite. Disaster struck the 49ers in the form of Giants defensive tackle Erik Howard breaking through and knocking the ball loose from Craig with a shot to his midsection. The ball rolled off Craig's hip and Lawrence Taylor swooped in to recover it. Giants quarterback Jeff Hostetler took over from there, driving into 49ers territory, where Bahr kicked a game-winning 42-yard field goal as time expired to quash the 49ers' dream of a three-peat. "This is a nightmare for running backs," a disconsolate Craig said after the game. "You think about keeping two hands on the ball as you run through the hole. You can't make excuses. I have to live with what I did."

Craig, who in 1985 had became the first player to have 1,000 yards rushing and receiving in the same season, never played for the 49ers again. The team let him go as a Plan B free agent before the start of the next season.

# "Super Bowl or Die"

In the midst of his audition at the San Francisco 49ers Santa Clara practice facility, free agent linebacker Gary Plummer noticed he was drawing a crowd. As Plummer went through his workout for pro personnel man Bill McPherson and linebackers coach John Marshall, general manager John McVay strolled out on the balcony overlooking the practice field. A steady procession of scouts, coaches, and administrative staff followed him onto the parapet until it became standing room only.

Plummer was just a little flabbergasted. He'd never experienced that kind of attention at any level or at any stage of a long, standout career. "They flew me up for what they deemed a little workout," Plummer said. "It ended up going for close to an hour, and as it was going on, more and more people kept coming out until that balcony was jammed. It was intimidating, yet impressive. I kind of chuckled to myself, 'This is your idea of a little workout?' But that was the importance they were placing on improving their defense. That was the importance they were placing on winning a championship."

Moving aggressively at the dawn of the salary cap era, the 49ers had, at the direction of team president Carmen Policy, restructured the contracts of several of their players to gain financial flexibility for a free-agent haul. Within days of his March 1994 workout, Plummer turned down the San Diego Chargers' bid to retain him in favor of becoming the first of a dozen free agents signed by the 49ers. The bounty included nine unrestricted free agents.

The parade of newcomers following Plummer was a star-laden bunch, none brighter than cornerback Deion Sanders. Dominic Corsell, the 49ers assistant director of football operations, said Sanders was so eager to play for the 49ers that he initiated contact with the team through his agent and quickly agreed to a $1 million salary. The pay was well below the market rate for a marquee pass defender.

Other unrestricted free agents signed were cornerback Toi Cook; defensive ends Richard Dent, Rickey Jackson, and Charles Mann; center Bart Oates; wide receiver Ed McCaffrey; and linebacker Ken Norton Jr. Norton's signing was especially gratifying to the 49ers. His fast, hard-nosed style play added fire and muscle to a unit looking to remake itself and shed its finesse image. At the same time, Norton's acquisition took him away from Dallas, which the 49ers figured could only help them in their all-out bid to dethrone the reigning league champions. Defensive tackle Rhett Hall, defensive end Tim Harris, and guard Rod Milstead rounded out the wave of veteran acquisitions by the 49ers.

Those twelve joined a roster already brimming with some of football's biggest names: quarterback Steve Young, wide receivers Jerry Rice and John Taylor, tight end Brent Jones, running back Ricky Watters, defensive tackle Dana Stubblefield, and safety Tim McDonald, who had joined the team as a free agent the previous season. "Coming in here, I was somewhat starstruck," said defensive tackle Bryant Young, who with fellow first-round pick fullback William Floyd broke into the 49ers starting lineup as a rookie in 1994. "But I knew I couldn't be mesmerized by their status because I had a job to do, too. I understood they were my teammates but that I was brought here for much the same reason they were—the 49ers wanted to get to the Super Bowl, and they wanted to get there now."

Still, the 49ers' glittering roster and history of winning masked a doubt-ridden self-image, dragged down by three playoff losses in a four-year stretch. In each case, the final defeat ended their season a step short of a return trip to the Super Bowl. In 1990 the 49ers had been denied a third consecutive Super Bowl berth when the New York Giants prevailed in the NFC title game. Then, reestablishing themselves as a 49ers nemesis, the Dallas Cowboys dealt San Francisco successive losses in NFC title games following the 1992 and 1993 seasons en route to back-to-back Super Bowl titles.

The 17-point conference championship loss to the Cowboys following the 1993 campaign was especially galling for team owner Eddie DeBartolo and club president Carmen Policy. In their minds it demonstrated that the gulf between the 49ers and Dallas had grown wider. "I don't think we could fathom going through that again," said Steve Young, who fell short in his first two tries to become the only 49ers quarterback besides Joe Montana to lead the team to an NFL title. "In a weird way, it was more painful to go to a championship game and lose than not to go to it at all. I guess the only thing more painful would be to go to the Super Bowl and lose."

Yet, it was in the final moments of that 38–21 loss at Texas Stadium that the determined—some might say desperate—course for the 49ers' coming redemption was formed. As DeBartolo and Policy rode the stadium elevator down to the visitors locker room to meet with the team, the club owner turned to Policy and told him in no uncertain terms that they couldn't let the Cowboys embarrass the 49ers again. Then, he told Policy to do whatever it took to overtake them. "From there they did everything they could do or thought they needed to do to see that it didn't happen again," said 49ers play-by-play man Joe Starkey.

Taking the words of his disconsolate owner to heart, Policy even took the 49ers' typical motto of "Super Bowl or bust" one step further. It was, as he would often say during the coming season, "Super Bowl or die."

So it was with this mindset and just over four minutes to go in the 1994 Monday night season opener that head coach George Seifert decided to take care of unfinished business. The 49ers were blowing out the Los Angeles Raiders 37–14. Jerry

*Jerry Rice is perhaps the greatest receiver in NFL history.*
Sports Gallery/Al Messerschmidt

Rice, who needed one more score to move ahead of Jim Brown's NFL record 126 career touchdowns, jogged back onto the field, joined by Steve Young and other 49ers starters.

Young huddled with his teammates and said, "We're taking our shot. Let's get Jerry the record right here." Rice bolted downfield on a post pattern. Dodging pressure, Young got off a pass that was slightly underthrown. Rice braked inside the 5, then out-jumped defensive backs Albert Lewis and Eddie Anderson for the ball before walking into the end zone past the fallen defenders for the milestone score. "I'm embarrassed it was a little short, but I was on my back and that was all I had," Young said afterward. "But it was perfect that it was a little short and that he had to go up and grab it and take it away from everybody. Maybe that's the way it should be."

To the chagrin of the Raiders, the record-breaking touchdown set off an end zone celebration. Left tackle Steve Wallace hustled down field and was right in the middle of it. "I was fortunate enough to be one of the first guys down there," said Wallace, who hoisted Rice with a congratulatory bear hug. "That was a record that had stood for twenty-nine years, and as a group we wanted to pick him up and show our appreciation."

Rice finished the night with 3 scores in a dazzling offensive display by the 49ers. It was all part of a Monday night effort, Wallace said, "to set the tone and let everyone in the nation know that—hey, we're for real, and this is the San Francisco 49ers' year."

But directly ahead lay one of the 49ers' most emotional games ever, a showdown in Kansas City with none other than former San Francisco quarterback Joe Montana and his new team. It was the latest installment of Joe versus Steve, the long-running quarterback controversy spawned in 1987, when then 49ers coach Bill Walsh pulled off the trade that brought the scrambling Young to San Francisco from Tampa Bay. Now, just a few months after settling on Young as the starter and trading their four-time Super Bowl winner to the Chiefs in a decision Policy likened to an emotional earthquake, the 49ers were competing against the hero of the NFL's "Team of the '80s."

Young, who spent four years as Montana's backup before establishing himself as the starter, desperately wanted to win. So did Montana and so did Seifert, who had risked a fan backlash by deciding to stick with Young as his quarterback rather than give the job back to Montana, who missed all of 1991 and most of 1992 with elbow problems.

At a packed, deafening Arrowhead Stadium, it would be Montana who got the better of his old team, with a big assist from linebacker Derrick Thomas. The Chiefs' extraordinary pass rusher, exploiting a banged-up 49ers offensive line, had 3 of the Chiefs' 4 sacks, including one of Young in the end zone for a safety that helped turn the tide in Kansas City's 24–17 victory. "It was a wild, crazy day," 49ers left tackle Steve Wallace said. "We all had so much respect for Joe Montana, but I can remember how much Steve wanted to win the game, and it was really big for George Seifert as well. The only problem was there was a guy named D. T. If you wanted to pick an MVP of the game, it was Derrick Thomas. He was rushing our quarterback so hard and so fast and smacking into him so much that his legs were cramping. They'd take him off to the sideline, give him some fluids, and back he'd come. I was praying, 'Please, God, let this guy keep cramping so he won't hit our quarterback any more.' It was an ugly sight."

Despite the pass-protection problems, the 49ers fought back to make it close. But cornerback David Whitmore, who was included in the trade that sent Montana to Kansas City, helped wrap up the win when he stopped a Young scramble in the fourth quarter with a touchdown-saving tackle. "It was an incredible day for Joe," Wallace said of Montana, who threw for a pair of touchdowns, including one to Joe Valerio on a tackle-eligible play. "On our end, there was disappointment. Whenever you're up against one of your former players, an ex-teammate, it's almost like you're in your back-yard again competing. You just always want to beat those guys."

Young couldn't beat Montana so he settled for learning from him again, telling reporters afterward, "In a lot of ways, it shows the master still had some more to teach the student."

The 49ers rebounded to put together consecutive wins, including a 24–13 victory over New Orleans that featured Sanders coming out as a defensive force with a 74-yard inter-ception return for a clinching touchdown. After picking off Jim Everett's pass in the late going, "Primetime" zigged right and zagged left before high-stepping over the last 30 yards. Seifert joked afterward that he'd fined Sanders $100 for prancing too soon. Seifert added he was paying the fine.

One week later, against Philadelphia at Candlestick Park, the 49ers' mood couldn't have been more different. The defense that had been assembled with such care, effort, and expense—the 49ers' remade unit featured seven new starters from the previous season—couldn't stop the Eagles' Randall Cunningham or running back Charlie Garner. And Eagles defensive lineman William Fuller was at the center of a ferocious pass rush that was putting one hit after another on Young. "It was almost surreal in the way it went," Young said.

# Victory Lap

As the 49ers huddled before running out the final seconds on the victory over Dallas that sent them to their fifth Super Bowl, the first without quarterback Joe Montana, tackle Steve Wallace emphatically began pointing at Steve Young, Montana's successor. The crowd at Candlestick Park picked up on the gesture. In a thundering chorus of appreciation, the fans began chanting, "Steve! Steve! Steve!" "In my view, I was getting the monkey off his back—well, at least halfway, anyway, because we still had to play the Super Bowl," Wallace said. "I was just saying, 'Appreciate this guy.' He's wanted this and worked for this and gone through a lot, and he's taking this team and everyone connected with it to the Super Bowl."

An ecstatic Young punctuated the 49ers' title-game win with a wild victory lap around the stadium, thrusting his arms up in triumph and slapping hands with fans along the way.

Indeed, it would be a game like no other during the 1994 campaign. The 49ers' 40–8 loss to the Eagles was, at the time, the worst since a 45-point loss at Dallas, 59–14, on October 12, 1980. There were even public rumblings about Seifert's job security after the disaster, including an impromptu poll by KGO radio, the 49ers' flagship station, in which a majority of respondents said they'd prefer Jimmy Johnson be the coach of the 49ers. "I'd like to thank the 15 percent who voted for me," Seifert cracked in a postpractice session with reporters.

While the magnitude of the loss was mind-boggling in the context of the 49ers' long-running success, a howling sideline blowup by the normally mild-mannered Young also marked the game as a defining moment. With the Eagles pummeling and pulling away from the 49ers, Seifert approached Young, Rice, and several others midway through the third quarter. "Look, I think this thing is over and I'm going to be taking you out," Seifert told them.

Still, when the 49ers got the ball back, Young, Rice, and the rest of the starting unit took the field. In the midst of the drive, after seeing Young get bashed again by the Eagles' Fuller, Seifert called time-out with 4:09 remaining in the third quarter and the 49ers trailing 33–8, and replaced Young with Elvis Grbac. Young thought that if he was going to be lifted, other starters would be leaving the field at the same time. When he was the only one replaced in the middle of a series, "I just thought, 'Come on. What are you doing?'"

By the time he reached the sideline, an infuriated Young was loaded for bear. In full view of television cameras, he began berating Seifert, who stood on the sideline stoically while his quarterback called him every name in the book. Ten years later, recalling the episode, Young said he owes a debt of gratitude to Seifert, first for looking out for his welfare and second for absorbing his profanity-laced tirade with uncommon grace. "I said things you should never say to another person," Young said, "and I'm grateful for George's patience. But for me, I think that let out a lot of pent-up emotions. I think I had had to swallow so much and really hadn't externalized a lot of it. I think it just came pouring out. I was looking for a fight. I was looking for someone to fight and no one would fight me."

For his part Seifert said he wouldn't have done anything differently, including the decision to yank Young out of the game at that moment after seeing him take one hit too many. "As a

## In the Shadows of Legends

**George Seifert knew what it was like to follow a legend, having succeeded future Hall of Famer Bill Walsh as the 49ers head coach in 1989. That's why he let quarterback Steve Young (Joe Montana's successor) vent his frustrations after being pulled from the 40–8 loss to the Eagles. "Don't think I didn't hear Steve behind me yelling," Seifert said. "It's an emotional game and Steve is an emotional player. There were times I lost it, too. But I understood the situation Steve was in because I was in a similar one. We didn't have a lot in common, but that was one thing on which we could relate."**

coach, though, taking him out was a pretty easy decision," he said. "In fact, it was a no-brainer. That was a game we weren't going to come back from. We had a lot of season left, and I didn't want to leave him in there to run around and get his butt knocked off."

In time Young and the 49ers would reap the benefits of Seifert's logic, and the team itself learned from the lopsided loss to the Eagles. "We had so much talent that for a while we felt we could just walk out on the field and win, so we needed that type of game," Wallace said. "It definitely was a slap in the face, an eye-opener for us."

However, there was a time that the 1994 season could have gone either way for the 49ers. Looking back, tight end Brent Jones believes that pivotal moment came a week after the Philadelphia disaster, when the 49ers were playing the Lions at the Pontiac Silverdome. "I remember being in the huddle, our proverbial backs against the walls, and everybody saying, 'Come

Quarterback Steve Young celebrates in the end zone during the 49ers NFC Championship Game victory in 1995.

Eric Risberg/AP

on, we've got to snap back. We've got pull out of this. Let's do it,'" Jones said. "And when we did I knew—we all knew—it was a turning point."

The game began ominously. With the 49ers down 7–0 in the first quarter, Young was sandwiched by three Detroit defenders and ridden into the turf. Grimacing from the pain but still playing with a chip on his shoulder after being pulled from the Eagles game, Young limped to the sideline, where he stayed for only two plays, before hobbling back out on the field.

Detroit would score again to go in front 14–0, and the 49ers, who were one loss from dropping to a .500 record six games into season, seemed to be teetering on disaster. Instead of going off the deep end, though, the 49ers rallied.

Young put together a second-quarter drive that Ricky Watters finished with a 4-yard sweep for a score, and rookie fullback William Floyd's short, tenacious touchdown run pulled the 49ers into a halftime tie.

As the 49ers readied to play the second half, safeties Merton Hanks and Tim McDonald huddled with their defensive team-mates, declaring the season was on the line and urging them to make a stand. "We've got to go out here and make a play," Hanks said repeatedly.

Hanks heeded his own call, intercepting Scott Mitchell's first pass of the third quarter and returning it 38 yards to Detroit's 7 yard line. A few moments later, Floyd determinedly burrowed through Detroit's defensive line for his second 1-yard touch-down run. He celebrated the 49ers' first lead by exultantly thumping his chest.

Hanks, continuing to play despite breaking his nose when he caught an elbow through his face mask from Barry Sanders, thwarted another Detroit drive with a fumble recovery. Later Young accounted for the last of 27 unanswered points by the 49ers when he threw a 5-yard touchdown pass to Nate Singleton. The 49ers won 27–21.

Sore and spent after the gritty effort, Young limped slowly off the field, turning to public relations director Rodney Knox and telling him, "You know, this is harder than I remember it. It's been a really hard start to the season." But Young also was starting to feel pretty good about where the 49ers were and where they could go. "For me, when we walked out of Detroit, it was like, 'Okay, we can do about anything,'" Young said. "The fact that we came back and won, and where we were the week before with the Philadelphia game, that's when I think we got our turbo boost."

The 49ers took off from there, stringing together a phenomenal run that would withstand a severe test from rival Dallas to become a ten-game winning streak. It remains the third-longest streak in the team's history.

## Mastering a Texas Two-Step

The question was intense, the answer emphatic. "Are you sure it will work?" Coach George Seifert demanded of his offensive coordinator, Mike Shanahan. "Yes, Coach, I'm sure. I'm absolutely sure," Shanahan replied.

The exchange occurred at the team's Santa Clara headquarters in the days leading up to the 49ers' November meeting with Dallas, the first since the Cowboys ended their season the previous January by beating them in the conference championship. Shanahan and Seifert were talking about a key element of the offensive coordinator's game plan—using Young to run quarterback bootlegs in a bid to get around the Cowboys' best defensive player, pass-rushing linebacker–defensive end Charles Haley.

Haley broke into the league with the 49ers in 1986 and helped the team win consecutive Super Bowls in the 1988 and 1989 seasons. A mercurial talent, Haley clashed with Seifert and once got in Young's face over his poor play in an ugly loss to the Los Angeles Raiders in 1991. A year later the 49ers traded Haley to Dallas, where he aided the Cowboys' successive championship runs while simultaneously helping to deny the 49ers' title bids.

Shanahan had noted that Haley's aggressive tactics included pinching hard to the inside. By faking a run up the middle to the tailback or fullback, Shanahan believed Haley could be drawn in and Young would be able to bootleg around left end for some big gains.

On a crisp, clear Sunday in November, game day turned his theory into reality. On the first series, Young scooted around Haley for a 25-yard gain. In the second quarter, Young ran around Haley again for an advance of 15 yards. A personal foul on the tackle moved the ball to Dallas's 12 yard line, and Young eventually would score on a sneak that tied the teams. "I think that might have been the most confused I'd ever seen Charles in his career," 49ers tight end Brent Jones said.

Just as Young's runs took the Cowboys by surprise, so did the ferocity of the 49ers' defensive play. Early on, linebacker Ken Norton leveled Emmitt Smith, standing over him and shaking his head, "Not today!" Linebacker Rickey Jackson followed with another bone-rattling takedown of Smith. The hits epitomized the kind of brutal physical play opposing teams would come to expect from San Francisco's revamped defense. "I think it kind of sent a message that we were there to play and play hard," said linebacker Gary Plummer.

With the score tied at 7–7 and 2:49 remaining in the second quarter, Smith ran a lead draw and was just getting ready to accelerate through the hole when Jackson knifed in from right end and leveled Smith with a crushing blow. The stunned Smith lay on the ground for some 30 seconds before getting to his feet and slowly jogging off the field. He would return but wouldn't be the same against a defense that seemed to coalesce around Jackson's hit as Plummer, Norton, and McDonald joined in to shut down Smith's running lanes.

Consider that Smith had run for 294 yards and 5 touchdowns in three straight wins over the 49ers, including the two NFC championship victories. He seemed to be rolling toward another big day before the jolts from Norton and Jackson. From then on, Smith gained only 26 yards on 11 carries.

With Dallas struggling to run and becoming preoccupied with the running of the 49ers' quarterback—Young finished with 60 yards on 8 carries—the 49ers went deep to Jerry Rice. He caught Young's 57-yard touchdown pass to give the 49ers a lead they wouldn't surrender.

The previous bootlegs figured in the 49ers' last touchdown, when Young threw a 13-yard scoring pass to Jones after faking a quarterback run. Jones's score gave the 49ers a 21–7 lead, and they went on to win 21–14. "People had started saying the Cowboys had our number and we couldn't beat them, so when we did, it was a huge lift for us," Jones said. "Clearly it wasn't a playoff game, but it gave us confidence that we could succeed later in the year against them. Really, from that point on, all everybody talked about was playing them again in the playoffs."

Both Dallas and the 49ers steamrolled subsequent opposition, staying on a collision course for a third straight meeting in the NFC Championship Game. The 49ers, who clinched home-field advantage with a 42–19 win over Denver on December 18, rolled past an overmatched Chicago Bears' squad with a 44–15 victory in the divisional playoffs, setting up another meeting with the Cowboys.

When the 1994 Pro Bowl selections came out, cornerback Eric Davis was the only member of the 49ers' secondary who didn't make it. He still went to Hawaii, though, at the insistence of his teammates. Safeties Tim McDonald and Merton Hanks and cornerback Deion Sanders told Davis they didn't want to go to the NFL's annual all-star game in Honolulu unless he came with them. So, Davis packed his bags and joined his friends.

It was a fitting reward for Davis. All year, he played the role of the steady, quietly reliable pass defender opposite the flashy Sanders, whose pizzazz and playmaking during a spectacular season earned him defensive player of the year honors. But with a Super Bowl berth on the line in the third straight NFC title game pitting the 49ers against Dallas, it would be Davis who took on the persona of a daring, swashbuckling defender.

On the game's third play, Davis gambled, slipping off Michael Irvin, the receiver he was supposed to cover, and cutting in front of Kevin Williams to intercept a Troy Aikman pass. Forty-four yards later, Davis was in the end zone, starting a 21-point spree in the opening minutes of the conference championship, all off Dallas turnovers. "He was baiting the guy,"

49ers defensive end Rickey Jackson said afterward. "That's just the way Deion would have done it."

"He's my partner in prime," is the way Sanders put it after the 49ers hung on to finally beat the Cowboys 38–28.

The interception was especially sweet for Davis, who had been scorched by Alvin Harper for a touchdown and a long pass that set up another score in the 49ers' successive conference championship losses to the Cowboys. "It was a calculated risk," Davis said. "I had my back to my receiver to make them think I was manned up on him. I made my break and just beat him to the ball."

Davis didn't stop there. On the ensuing series, he stripped the ball from Irvin, and McDonald recovered the fumble, leading to Steve Young's 29-yard touchdown pass to Ricky Watters. On the subsequent kickoff, Adam Walker forced a fumble by return man Kevin Williams, and kicker Doug Brien recovered, setting up a third score on William Floyd's 1-yard touchdown run. The 49ers had a 21–0 lead with 7:33 left in the first quarter.

Dallas mounted a comeback, but the 49ers kept up the pressure. Young hit Rice with a 28-yard touchdown pass and later ran for a 3-yard score, lunging over the goal line for the touchdown. The 49ers registered 3 of their 4 sacks in the fourth quarter, fending off a gallant Cowboys' comeback. At last the 49ers had sent home the team that had ended their season in each of the last two years. Only surprise AFC-champion San Diego remained between them and their first Super Bowl title since the 1988 and 1989 teams had won successive championships.

As 49ers owner Eddie DeBartolo received the conference championship trophy in a postgame ceremony on the muddy Candlestick Park field, he vowed the team would deliver a final victory. "We are going to go to Miami and we are going to bring back another championship," DeBartolo said.

# Five for Five

They rest in a shimmering glass case in the lobby of the 49ers' Santa Clara headquarters, silent sentinels to the team's uncommon history of perfection in the National Football League's greatest game. From 1981 to 1994 the 49ers went to the NFC Championship Game nine times. They advanced to the Super Bowl on five occasions and emerged from each of those five title matches as the last team standing, coming home with the Vince Lombardi Trophy emblematic of the NFL's champion.

The 49ers were the first team to win five Super Bowls and remain the only club with multiple appearances in the Super Bowl to post an undefeated record. Their success has coincided with the team's lofty expectations that preceded each season and became incorporated into what players called the "49ers Way."

"I want to say this is our standard," said Steve Young, who was the MVP in the 49ers' last Super Bowl victory following the 1994 season. When it comes to the 49ers' play in the Super Bowl, it was a gold standard.

## Super Bowl XVI: A Cinderella Story

Days before the first Super Bowl in the 49ers' history—game XVI to crown the NFL champion for 1981—Bill Walsh, the team's cerebral, demanding coach, became a prankster. Walsh had attended a banquet in Washington, D.C., honoring him as coach of the year, and he flew on his own to Detroit, arriving at the 49ers' hotel a couple of hours before the team. He decided to greet the players as one of the hotel employees, giving $20 to a bellhop to let him use his uniform. "I don't know where I got the idea from, but I knew we all needed to loosen up, including me," Walsh said.

The sight of the white-haired Walsh in the bellhop's outfit trying to carry the bags of his players remains one of the enduring images leading up to the 49ers' Super Bowl meeting with the Cincinnati Bengals on January 24, 1982, at the Pontiac Silverdome. "I went up to Joe Montana, and he wouldn't give me his bag," Walsh said with a laugh. A couple of other players turned away his offers to take their baggage and entreaties for a

# "We Wanted to Be Champions"

**Running back Bill Ring and his teammates were paying close attention to Jack "Hacksaw" Reynolds because the hard-hitting linebacker and defensive leader rarely spoke up in team meetings. As the 49ers' first Super Bowl (XVI) neared, Reynolds stood before the gathering of his teammates, reached into his pocket, and pulled out a ring that he never wore. He had received it as a member of the NFC-champion Los Angeles Rams, who lost to the Pittsburgh Steelers in the Super Bowl two years earlier.**

**"He told us, 'You don't want this. This is like the booby prize,'" Ring said. "We laughed, but it hit home with me and I think with all of us. It was like, 'Why go for the crumbs?' We wanted to be champions, nothing less."**

tip before defensive tackle Lawrence Pillars finally recognized him, and the entire team began to crack up. "It was just something I wanted to do to lighten the mood, and ease the stress and pressure," Walsh said.

Walsh's comedy act broke the tension, at least for a while, and the 49ers plunged into their Super Bowl week workouts with a sense of confidence and calm. They would need every bit of both to weather the challenge from the Bengals.

Kenny Loggins's "This Is It" blared in the locker room as the 49ers readied to play Cincinnati. Joe Montana had selected the song, and Dwight Hicks made sure everyone heard it by having the volume turned up full blast.

The 49ers took the field, fired up by their music and its message. They heard Diana Ross's stirring rendition of the national anthem, and then whooped it up on the sideline when they won the coin toss, electing to receive the ball. Their excitement gave way to seriousness in a hurry.

Amos Lawrence fielded the opening kickoff and returned it 17 yards before he was hit hard and fumbled, giving the Bengals a first down at the 49ers' 26 yard line. "Our whole bench, our whole sideline went quiet—it was like a deflating balloon," Hicks, the 49ers safety, recalled. "For some reason, I jumped up and I said, 'Hell, no! It's time to play now. Let's go.'" So began the 49ers' first sequence from scrimmage and a telling moment in a game that would be defined by two defensive stands.

Cincinnati quarterback Ken Anderson completed 3 consecutive passes to move the ball to the 5 yard line before linebacker Willie Harper stopped Charles Alexander for no gain and defensive end Jim Stuckey broke through to sack Anderson for a 6-yard loss. On third down from the 11, Anderson threw toward the goal line for Isaac Curtis, but Hicks swooped in for the interception, denying the Bengals points and giving the 49ers field position with a return to the 32. "I wanted to be the one to make the plays because that's how I was measured as a player," Hicks said. "But that wasn't just me. I was able to intercept that pass because of the scheme we were in and the work of our defensive front. But most important to me was what we did as a defense under those circumstances. When things are going in your favor, anybody can play well. It's how you react in the face of adversity, how you respond, and I had the good fortune with the help of my teammates to make that play."

Hicks remembers O. J. Simpson seeking him out after the game, telling him, "Dwight, I don't know if anybody told you, but that play you made was the biggest in the game." It did produce an immediate swing in the 49ers' favor. With Bill Walsh calling a beautiful mix of runs and passes, and Joe Montana coolly executing the plays, the 49ers moved 68 yards for a touchdown. Montana got the last yard, slicing into the end zone between center Fred Quillan and guard Randy Cross.

Another takeaway—this one coming when cornerback Eric Wright stripped the ball from Cris Collinsworth—set up the next 49ers' touchdown, and two Ray Wersching field goals put San Francisco up 20–0 at halftime. But the 49ers would need another defensive stand to fend off a gallant Bengals team. Cincinnati opened the second half by driving for a touchdown and, after making some halftime adjustments, the Bengals defenders twice held the 49ers without a first down, forcing punts.

Following the second punt, the Bengals took over at midfield. On a third-and-11 play from the 15, Anderson hit tight end Dan Ross with a 10-yard pass. Defensive coordinator Chuck Studley brought in the goal line defense when the Bengals opted to go for the first down, and their hulking fullback Pete Johnson got it with a 2-yard burst up the middle.

The Bengals, trailing by 13 late in the third quarter, now had first-and-goal at the 3 yard line. Johnson hit the center of the line but was stopped a yard shy of the end zone when he was stood up by the defensive front and linebackers Hacksaw Reynolds and Dan Bunz before Fred Dean swept in from the side to knock him down. Johnson tried the middle again. He was held for no gain when the 49ers front, augmented by defensive tackle John Harty and John Choma, who normally played offensive line, got

Running back Earl Cooper runs through the Bengals defense in Super Bowl XVI.
AP

the jump on the Bengals line. They closed down the running lanes with Reynolds, Bunz, and Keena Turner along with Ronnie Lott rushing in to fill in the gaps.

Facing third-and-goal, Anderson swung a pass out to Charles Alexander. Bunz, anticipating what was to come, ran toward him and slammed his helmet in the running back's chest the instant he caught the ball, stopped him cold in a touchdown-saving one-on-one tackle. "Dan recognized that play and made a picture-perfect tackle and thwarted his momentum," Hicks said. "If he hit him any other way or a little bit later, his momentum would have carried him into the end zone."

The Bengals gave it one last try, but Reynolds led the fourth-down defensive charge, slamming shut the center gap as the rest of his teammates swarmed around Johnson to stop him for no gain. "I was kind of dazed but I remember seeing Ronnie Lott throwing his arms in the air and everybody started to jump around and I knew, 'Whoa, we stopped them!'" Bunz said. "That stand was the ultimate team effort because one guy weakens or cracks, they would have pushed through. When we held them, I think that kind of broke their will. They were shocked, I think, almost like, 'How could this happen?'"

To their credit, the Bengals regrouped to score another touchdown, but the 49ers answered with a long drive ending in a field goal by Wersching for a 9-point cushion. With time running low, Anderson threw a pass to Collinsworth that was intercepted by Wright, leading to another Wersching field goal. With 20 seconds left, Anderson threw a short touchdown pass to Ross but Jim Breech's onside kick was covered by Dwight Clark. The 49ers secured their first championship, using their offense to get there and their defense to bring it home in a 26–21 win.

# Super Bowl XIX: Back in the Game

In the aftermath of the 49ers' dominating 38–16 victory over favored Miami in Super Bowl XIX at Stanford Stadium, Dolphins quarterback Dan Marino sat in the locker room and answered the postgame questions until there were no more. Then he and a friend, Dolphins wide receiver Jimmy Cefalo, got into a waiting limousine. As they were slowly driven away through a gauntlet of taunting 49ers fans, Marino reached for the chilled bottle of champagne left for him in anticipation of victory. "Jimmy," he said as he popped the cork and poured the drinks, "Did we get our asses kicked or what?"

The 49ers' 38–16 beating of Don Shula's high-flying Dolphins marked San Francisco's second championship in four years after going its first thirty-one years in the National Football League without one. It was a game the 49ers, who rolled through the playoffs and won fifteen of their sixteen regular-season games, were sure they could win even before taking the field against the Dolphins. "When you have a year like we did, that generated a powerful feeling amongst us that it wasn't a matter of whether we were going to win, but by how much," 49ers offensive lineman Randy Cross said.

The game's 22-point margin didn't even reflect the 49ers' dominance in the game. Roger Craig had a field day, scoring three times in a game that saw the 49ers rack up 537 yards in offense and average 7.1 yards per play against the Dolphins' overmatched defense. With Miami's linebackers and safeties chasing Craig and Wendell Tyler in pass coverage, the field was left wide open for the quarterback to run. And Montana took full advantage, scrambling downfield five times for 59 yards, setting up a couple touchdowns along the way.

"We just knew those guys weren't going to stop us," Cross recalled. "With Roger and Wendell and Freddie Solomon and Dwight Clark and Joe, we had too many weapons. And as a group, they were a less physical team, especially on defense. In the NFC, we had beaten tough, physical teams like the Chicago Bears and New York Giants to get there, and the Dolphins just didn't match up well with us."

The mismatch was just as great on the other side of the ball, where Miami's offensive juggernaut never really got off the ground against the 49ers, and faltered completely in the second half, when the Dolphins failed to score. Though the Dolphins used a no-huddle with some limited success in the first half, they were never able to run the 49ers out of their nickel defense. That allowed San Francisco's defensive linemen to tee off on Marino even as Tom Holmoe and Jeff Fuller were on the field as extra defensive backs. "We had such great athletes and guys who could hit and tackle that they weren't going to beat us even if they tried to run," said safety Dwight Hicks.

Marino wound up throwing 50 times. Montana had more passing yardage (331) on 15 fewer throws (35) than the Miami quarterback, who was sacked three times on the first six plays of the second half, twice by Dwaine Board.

When it did begin to look as if the Dolphins finally were beginning to move, Marino, who had thrown a record 48 touchdown passes in the regular season, shot a pass to the end zone for Mark Clayton that cornerback Eric Wright stretched out to intercept. "I can't really describe how it all happened, but I do know if I don't make a play on that ball, it's a touchdown," Wright said. "I consider it one of the better plays I ever made in my career, just because of what it meant for our team and the game that it came in."

Safety Carlton Williamson put the finishing touches on the second-half shutout with an assist from Hicks. Anticipating a pass play because of the formation the Dolphins were in, Hicks convinced Williamson to shift his alignment and make it appear he was coming off coverage of tight end Joe Rose to guard Hicks' man, Nathan Moore. But once the play began, Hicks stayed with Moore and Williamson hung with Rose. Marino tried to get the ball to Rose, but Williamson hustled into position to make the interception in front of the tight end in the end zone. The play had unfolded as Hicks had told him in the moments before the snap.

"How did you know?" Williamson asked as Hicks congratulated him in the end zone.

"Because," Hicks said simply, "I study."

## Super Bowl XXIII: The Legend of Joe Cool

There they were, on their own 8 yard line and trailing the Cincinnati Bengals 16–13 with time running out in Super Bowl XXIII at Miami's Joe Robbie Stadium. Center Randy Cross set up the 49ers huddle in their own end zone. To take the lead, they'd have to go 92 yards against a defense that had stifled them most of the day.

Joe Montana came into the huddle with not a word to his teammates about the championship stakes. "He told us a couple jokes," 49ers wide receiver John Taylor said. "Then he goes,

'Hey, look. Turn around. There's John Candy.' Sure enough, John Candy was sitting there in the first row." Suddenly, the tension didn't seem so thick, the anxiety eased. Montana's words and action, in a way, provided the 49ers a light moment in the firestorm of football's grandest stage. And it gently reinforced, at a most critical time in a most critical game, that players play football best when they're loose and having fun.

"What Joe did was make the situation lighter than what it really was," Taylor said. "We were behind and we had to go down and score or lose, and Joe made it easier on us by taking pressure off, making it seem like we were in practice or playing in our backyard."

Said fullback Tom Rathman, "That was the type of personality and character he had in the huddle. He wanted everybody to keep their cool and we all knew with Mister Joe Cool back there, we were going to get it done. Everybody was poised. Nobody felt pressure."

The drive began with short, quick passes. Montana passed to running back Roger Craig for an 8-yard advance and then hit tight end John Frank for 7 yards and a first down. Jerry Rice, who won the Super Bowl MVP after finishing with 11 catches for a record 215 yards receiving, caught a 7-yarder next before runs by Craig netted 4 yards to take the clock down to the two-minute warning.

They would be the only runs during the 11-play march, unlike the last-ditch drive in the 1981 NFC title game, when Bill Walsh successfully used runs for significant yardage against Dallas's nickel defensive alignment. But the passes were controlled, high-percentage, low-risk plays designed to move the ball down the field in bits and chunks. "We moved the ball methodically," Rathman said. "It was about dinking and dunking, timing and precision. We took what they gave us and Joe did a great job of orchestrating the drive."

"It was the West Coast offense at its best," Craig said.

"Joe was popping the ball around to different people, keeping everybody involved," Taylor added. "Nobody was standing around, nobody had time to get caught up in the awe of the game. We were going right down the field and it was more so, 'This is what we've got to do, and let's go do it.'"

Completions of 17 and 27 yards to Rice and 13 and 8 yards to Craig around a penalty for illegal man downfield got the 49ers to the Bengals' 10 yard line with 39 seconds left. There was a time-out, and Walsh and Montana talked it over on the sideline. The second-down call was "Red Right Tight-F Left-20 HB Curl-X Up," a pass play Walsh had installed into the offense just the week before. "We actually ran the play wrong but it worked out right," Taylor said.

Roger Craig was supposed to go into motion toward the strong side, where Taylor was lined up like a tight end and Rice had moved into position as a flanker. But when Craig went into motion, he went toward the weak side. A Cincinnati linebacker followed him, though, leaving one less defender to clutter the field where the 49ers' wideouts would be working. "Roger took that man out of the picture, and I think that opened it up," Taylor said.

On the strong side, Rathman released into the flat, Rice bolted to the corner of the end zone, and Taylor ran a pattern akin to a skinny post, running up to the outside shoulder of the safety before cutting back across him and turning upfield.

The 49ers celebrate after their winning touchdown in Super Bowl XXIII.
Rusty Kennedy/AP

It happened quickly. As Taylor broke upfield, Montana threw the pass to him. Taylor looked back, saw the ball coming, and latched onto it as he crossed the goal line with 34 seconds remaining. He punctuated the dramatic score with a one-handed spike of the ball through his legs.

After the game, Taylor recalled his younger brother, Keith—who would go on to play in the NFL as well—congratulating him in the locker room. "He says to me, 'Man, how did you feel making that catch?'" Taylor said. "I told him I really hadn't even thought about that. And he says, 'Well, it's a good thing you caught it, because if you hadn't, you would have been the loneliest person in the world and probably unemployed.'"

There's no danger of that for Taylor when he looks back on one of the 49ers' pivotal moments. "I can say for the rest of my life I made a catch that won a Super Bowl," Taylor said. "That's something nobody can take away from you."

That includes the ball. Taylor retrieved it and later gave it as a keepsake to his parents. It remains at the family's home.

## Super Bowl XXIV: Post Time

Usually 49ers public relations director Jerry Walker made his way from the press box to the field with a few minutes left in every game to walk off with the coach and players and help arrange postgame interview sessions. There was no early press box exit during Super Bowl XXIV at the Louisiana Super Dome in New Orleans. "I got stuck in the NFL control room going over all the records we were shattering," Walker said.

San Francisco's 55–10 victory over the Denver Broncos on January 28, 1990, included the biggest victory margin in the

## Trash Talk

With some time on their hands following a practice the week of
Super Bowl XXIV against the Denver Broncos, 49ers wide receiver
John Taylor and defensive end Larry Roberts walked through the
French Quarter and stopped at a restaurant to get a bite to eat.
Inside, Taylor said, they ran into Denver running back Bobby
Humphrey and several other Broncos.

"They started talking trash, saying what they were going to do
to us and we weren't going to be able to do anything to stop
them. We didn't really say anything back to them talking. But we
talked about what happened with our team, and we all decided
that we weren't going to get in a war of words. We just said, 'We'll
do our talking and example-making come game time.'"

The approach proved to be a sound course, because it was the
49ers who got in the last word, and it was an emphatic one at that.

game's history: most points, most touchdowns (8), and, in Joe
Montana, the first three-time Super Bowl MVP. The 49ers won
their second straight Super Bowl in George Seifert's first season
as coach and became the first team since the Pittsburgh Steelers
in 1979 and 1980 to win back-to-back NFL championships. "I
think we came down here with a mission. We were very determined," Montana said after helping to cement the 49ers'
standing as the "Team of the '80s" by leading the club to its
fourth Super Bowl triumph of the decade.

San Francisco blew out Denver with one of the most
common pass routes in football, the post route—a staple in the
offensive, and defensive, playbook of most every team. Half of
the 49ers' 8 touchdowns were scored on post routes, with Jerry

*Jerry Rice shakes off a
defender in Super Bowl XXIV.*
Ed Reinke/AP

Rice catching 3 from Montana and John Taylor catching the fourth. Their first score, a 20-yard touchdown pass from Montana to Rice, finished their opening series and foreshadowed the success the 49ers would enjoy running the post.

Rice came open as he made his break and sprinted down the middle of the field. Montana fired the pass to Rice, who caught it inside the 10 yard line. Denver safety Steve Atwater, sensing he could put a lick on Rice that might knock him out of the game, closed in to take his shot. But he didn't get the knockdown that he wanted. Rice staggered but kept his feet and went in for the score, starting the 49ers' avalanche of points. "I tried to take him out right there," Atwater said after the game. "I should have just gone for the sure tackle."

Rice knew that Atwater was taking dead aim at him. "He really wanted to knock me down, but I tried to focus in on the ball and keep my balance and get into the end zone," Rice said.

The 49ers did mix it up, scoring on a pass from Montana to tight end Brent Jones and the first of 2 short touchdown runs by fullback Tom Rathman before returning to the post. Rice caught a 38-yarder just before halftime, and Rice and Taylor each caught third-quarter scoring passes after interceptions of Elway by safety Chet Brooks and linebacker Michael Walter. "They left a lot of open area in the middle and Joe read it every time," Rice said.

## Super Bowl XXIX: A Perfect Ending

George Seifert was seething. The 49ers coach was letting his players have it at a meeting in Miami just five days before the team was to meet the underdog San Diego Chargers in Super Bowl XXIX at Joe Robbie Stadium. He was upset and angered after learning that about a dozen of his players had missed curfew the night before. "George basically went off on the whole team," 49ers tackle Steve Wallace recalled. "He said, 'Hey, we're here getting ready to go for a world championship.'"

As soon as the flummoxed Seifert stomped out of the room, wide receiver Jerry Rice got into a heated exchange with cornerback Deion Sanders, who'd been among the players breaking curfew. Teammates stepped between the two to prevent them from coming to blows.

Rice had successfully argued for an hour-long extension of the curfew and was upset some of his teammates violated it. Sanders had objected to the curfew, viewing it as childish and unnecessary and arguing that in any other week, it would have been the regular player's day off anyway. Each player had his supporters.

Finally, with tensions between Rice and Sanders running high, Wallace stood up and addressed his teammates to try to defuse the situation. "Guys, come on," said Wallace, one of the team captains. "You know George had to go off on us at some point. He's looking at us and thinking we're too relaxed, everybody's having too good a time. We're big favorites and he's thinking if we don't watch it, we could have a New York Jets/Baltimore Colts–type game [Super Bowl III] where there's a huge upset. This was just his way of reminding us there's a reason and a purpose to why we're down here."

As Wallace's words seeped in, the tension in the meeting room seemed to dissipate. And later, on the practice field, it was all togetherness, on both sides of the ball. "From that point on, I think guys regained their focus," Wallace said. "We just had

# Foregone Conclusion

About an hour before the Super Bowl XXIX kickoff, Jerry Rice spotted linebacker Gary Plummer getting ready to play in his first Super Bowl, and the veteran wide receiver delivered an impromptu confidence booster. "Hey, tonight I'm going to get you your first Super Bowl ring," Rice told the first-year 49er.

"I'll never forget it because Jerry was so matter of fact," Plummer said. "I called my wife right after that and told her to have our boys at the 50 yard line with two minutes left and be ready to celebrate because we were going to kick butt."

these great practices, I would even say perfect practices, no dropped balls, no missed assignments."

Added tight end Brent Jones, "We had some practices that were just scary. I don't know if the ball ever touched the ground."

Even offensive coordinator Mike Shanahan, who usually ended practices with an informal critique, was left dumbfounded. "Mike had nothing to say except, 'Wow, you guys are ready to play,'" Wallace said.

It wasn't just the offense. Equally impressive were the fiercely efficient practices of the 49ers defense under coordinator Ray Rhodes. Linebacker Gary Plummer said the mushrooming defensive intensity had less to do with the team-meeting brouhaha than the championship desire simmering in the team's young players and long-suffering vets who joined the 49ers specifically for the chance to win a Super Bowl. "That meeting might have been a motivational flashpoint for the offense, but for a lot

*Steve Young hugs the
Lombardi Trophy following
Super Bowl XXIX.*
Eric Risberg/AP

of others it was just an interesting sidelight," Plummer said. "Defensively we had some near-perfect practices even before that, and we had a lot of guys who had championship motivations of their own."

Still, the 49ers' flawless Super Bowl week preparations were enough to leave Shanahan brimming with confidence. "When you have that type of practice, you know good things are going to happen during the game," Shanahan said. The 49ers would prove him right in a flash. They scored just one minute and 24 seconds into the Super Bowl and went on to win 49–26.

Even before the game, as the noise and smoke dissipated from the dazzling fireworks show and military flyover, Seifert glanced at the Chargers' sideline. What he saw filled him with confidence in the 49ers in the minutes before they began playing for their second Super Bowl title in his eight-year tenure as coach. "Their players," he said, "almost seemed in awe of all the hoopla. Our players seemed to me to just be getting ready for another game. Honestly, I believe they were distracted. We came out, and we came out explosively, and I really think they were still gathering themselves."

Shanahan was so sure the 49ers would beat the Chargers to the punch that he had told quarterback Steve Young he expected him to lead the team to its first touchdown within the game's first five plays. "I just felt like we were better than they were," Shanahan said. "Steve was so good at going through his progression. It was just like a guy that you would say, 'Hey, he's wired in.' Steve had worked his whole life for this opportunity, and you just saw during the week that there was no way he was not going to go out and have a great game."

As it turned out, Young beat Shanahan's expectation, connecting for a touchdown with Jerry Rice on the 49ers' third play from scrimmage. Rice raced downfield on a post pattern, split the Chargers safeties, and caught Young's pass in stride for a 44-yard touchdown. About 90 seconds later, after a San Diego punt, the 49ers got the ball back. This time Young scrambled for a big gain before using a play-fake to fullback William Floyd to freeze the Chargers secondary for an instant and hit running back Ricky Watters downfield for a 51-yard touchdown. "We felt like every time we touched the ball, we were going to score," guard Jesse Sapolu said. "It was like a symphony Steve Young was conducting, and everybody was just doing their job."

Young finished with a Super Bowl record 6 touchdown passes, surpassing the 5 his predecessor, Joe Montana, had in the 49ers' 55–10 victory over Denver in Super Bowl XXIV. "He made all the right decisions and all the right throws, and I was so happy for him because he got that monkey off his back that most people have when you follow a great player," Shanahan said. "He just prepared himself so well and he had such passion to win a Super Bowl."

Young, named the Super Bowl MVP, seconded that. As he celebrated the 49ers' 23-point victory over the Chargers on the sideline, he yelled, to no one in particular, "Take that monkey off my back!" Linebacker Gary Plummer obliged, coming over and figuratively lifting the weight off his shoulders. "There was a calming factor to it," Young said of realizing his long-sought championship quest. "It was like, 'Okay, we got there.' It makes a difference—it does."

Young by no means did it alone, getting loads of help from his teammates, including Rice, who caught 3 touchdown passes. Two of his scoring catches came after he separated a shoulder when he was taken down hard after a second-quarter reception. Battling flu-like symptoms that day, Rice also had been administered fluids intravenously before the Super Bowl to combat dehydration. "Nothing was going to keep me out of that game, I wanted to win so badly," Rice said after his 10-catch, 149-yard Super Bowl performance. "We all were brought together to do a job. We did it."

Deion Sanders and Toi Cook, who were among the free agents signed to rebuild the defense, each had interceptions along with Eric Davis, who was among the defensive holdovers. Helping to bottle up the Chargers' attack was safety Tim McDonald, who finished with 9 tackles in addition to knocking away 2 passes.

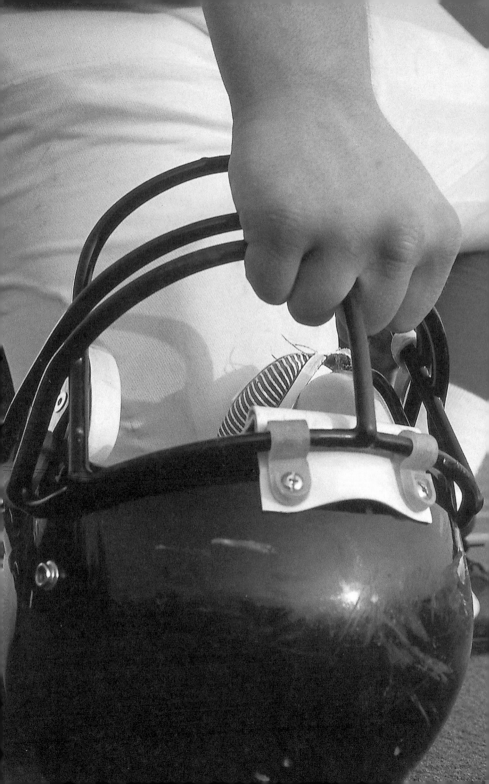

# Transitions

The laundry cart was brimming with gloves, game balls, shoes, helmets, and jerseys—some of the accoutrements of Jerry Rice's brilliant sixteen-year career with the 49ers. Without a word, assistant equipment manager Nick Pettit pushed the cart through the lobby of the team's Santa Clara headquarters and past the case holding the team's Super Bowl trophies, which included three that Rice helped to win. Out into the night he went, stopping when he got to Rice's car. Rice, holding an armful of shoe boxes, was right behind, trailed by 49ers security man Dario Montenegro and fellow wide receiver Terrell Owens, who had been in the midst of a solo nighttime workout at the team facility.

It was June 2001 and, just a few hours earlier, the 49ers had released Rice, cutting the NFL's greatest receiver and the last link to their Super Bowl winning teams of the 1980s. The salary cap-driven exit—orchestrated by former general manager Bill Walsh and finally executed by his successor, Terry Donahue—had stretched out over six months. It began with a public goodbye following the 49ers' last home game of the 2000 season. Rice, his uniform streaked with dirt and grass stains and his face streaked with tears, bade farewell to the Candlestick Park crowd from atop a hastily erected stage at midfield. "Guys," Rice said, "it's time for me to go. But San Francisco, I'll always love you guys."

Then teammates Terry Jackson and Winfred Tubbs hoisted Rice on their shoulders. Tackles Derrick Deese and Scott Gragg joined them, leaning in from opposite sides to provide additional support. Atop the slow-moving, chaotic scarlet and gold procession, Rice was carried off the field in a tribute to one of the greatest 49ers.

Now, as Rice, Pettit, Montenegro, and Owens piled the receiver's keepsakes into Rice's car and jammed them into the trunk, the emotion and finality of his 49ers' departure was hitting home. Rice gave Pettit and Montenegro farewell hugs, thanking each of them for helping him through his years with the team. Then he turned and shook hands with Owens.

Suddenly, Rice began rummaging through the car's trunk, pulled out one of his prized game balls, and gave it to his fellow

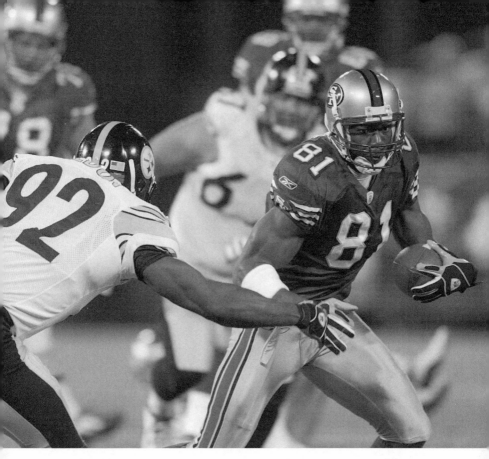

*Terrell Owens (81) succeeded Jerry Rice as the 49ers premier pass catcher.*
Joe Robbins

wide receiver. The gift to Owens was the ball Rice received from the team when he played against the Chicago Bears in his last home game as a 49er, the same game in which Owens upstaged Rice with an NFL-record 20 receptions. "It's kind of hard to get inside Jerry's mind, so I don't know what he was thinking," said Owens, who, among others, had had his differences with Rice. "But I know it means a lot to me. Despite all the things we went through, he's like a brother to me. I know it's hard for him to leave, and that's probably getting to him."

Rice walked to the driver's side door and squeezed into the seat behind the wheel, just about the only place where the bits and pieces of his career hadn't been stuffed into the car. "I'm done here," Rice said in a near whisper to a reporter who happened on the scene. "I'm at peace, and I'm ready to move on." With a slight smile and a wave goodbye, Rice drove away into the night. He didn't look back.

Jerry Rice had played against the Chicago Bears on December 17, 2000, knowing it would be his final home game as a 49er. As he looked at the many new faces in the locker room afterward, he also couldn't help thinking about the many players who were no longer there, and that he'd soon be joining them.

In many respects the departure of Rice signified the final element in the fall of the 49ers after twenty years at or near the top since the team's first Super Bowl title following the 1981 season. The walls did not come crumbling down all at once for the 49ers. The end came slowly and insidiously, drawn out over an agonizing two-year time frame that saw some sixty players come and go.

Elements coinciding with the team's decline also included an ownership feud that divided brother and sister. In addition, paralyzing salary-cap problems hastened the departures of some of the best 49ers and crippled the team's ability to adequately replace them. Safeties Tim McDonald and Merton Hanks, line-backer Ken Norton, guard Kevin Gogan, all past Pro Bowl players, were among the players let go by the 49ers as part of a cap-driven exodus.

All of that, though, was set in motion by a devastating hit in the Arizona desert that forced the premature retirement of Steve Young. The 49ers management team of club president Carmen

Policy and general manager Dwight Clark had long believed their annual go-for-broke tactics in the 1990s would reap dividends as long as Young was around. They reasoned the 49ers always had a chance to go to the Super Bowl provided Young had a good supporting cast, and the team's 1994 championship season was a case in point.

But the linchpin of that policy was about to break. When Eddie DeBartolo became ensnared in a gambling fraud probe in Louisiana in late 1997, he withdrew as the managing co-owner of the team. Day-to-day control of the 49ers was turned over to his co-owner sister, Denise DeBartolo York, and her husband, John York.

A short time later, Policy, who had expected to receive a minority stake in the team, had a falling out with ownership. He resigned as club president in the opening days of the 49ers' 1998 summer training camp. Policy went on from there to help organize the Cleveland Browns expansion franchise for owner Al Lerner.

Dwight Clark, who had remained with the 49ers as a front-office employee since retiring as a player in 1987, resigned as the general manager midway through the season to join Policy in Cleveland. "You see those office windows up there?" coach Steve Mariucci said, pointing to the team's second-story executive suites following a practice soon after Clark left. "There's nobody behind them." It fell to Mariucci to hold the team together, along with former general manager John McVay, who came out of retirement to help stabilize the front office during the second half of the 1998 campaign.

The 49ers managed to keep the festering management problems at bay during the 1998 season. They persevered through the losses of key executives and a lack of direction from the feuding owners to win ten or more games for the seventeenth time since 1981 and advance to the divisional playoffs. That's where they narrowly lost to Atlanta, the eventual NFC Super Bowl representative, after star running back Garrison Hearst fractured his left ankle on his first run of the game. "That's something I think about a lot," said Hearst. "If I never would have been injured, I truly believe we would have been capable of going all the way. We were just so good that year. Nobody had really stopped us all year. We were just so well balanced. We were committed to the run and Steve was throwing the ball with the best of them."

That proved to be the last gasp of the 49ers' tottering dynasty. Three weeks into the 1999 season at Arizona during a Monday-night game, 49ers running back Lawrence Phillips missed a blitz pickup, and cornerback Aeneas Williams stormed in unchecked to level Young. The collision knocked Young backward, and, as he fell, his head hit tackle Dave Fiore's leg before slamming into the ground.

Young lay unconscious for several seconds, and tackle Derrick Deese tugged at his jersey to try to help him up. Deese waved to the sideline for help, and team trainers and doctors ran onto the field, along with Mariucci. After a few more moments, Young came to, and walked off the field under his own power. He put on a baseball cap on and watched from the sideline as Jeff Garcia finished the game in his place. At one point Young tried to talk Mariucci into letting him go back in, but the coach would have none of it.

A few days later, Young recounted what he remembered of the frightening collision that ended his career. "I was shocked, that was my sense of it. I was just shocked," Young said "I remember a flash and as I was going backwards, catching Dave Fiore's knee and then the ground. And then mostly just resting for a second because I wanted to collect myself. But once I stood up, I felt I knew exactly what was going on, and that's why my initial reaction was to go back into the game."

The concussion was the fourth in three years for Young, who sat out the rest of the season before announcing in June 2000 that he was retiring.

The 49ers collapsed after the loss of Young, losing eleven of thirteen games to finish the year at 4–12, the worst since the 1979 team went 2–14 in Bill Walsh's first year as coach. A number of high-profile and high-salaried players were let go in the ensuing months as a new management team reigned in runaway salary-cap costs and complained that the previous regime had in effect "mortgaged" the team's future. Both Walsh, who returned in January 1999 as the 49ers general manager, and Mariucci pleaded for patience. "We're building a team" was a common refrain heard from both men.

And it would be the York family that would oversee the construction. As part of a settlement of dueling lawsuits in the spring of 2000, Eddie DeBartolo and Denise DeBartolo York split the family's $1 billion-plus financial empire. The Yorks wound up with sole possession of the 49ers, an ownership transfer that was approved in a vote of NFL owners in May of 2000. DeBartolo, who had been so closely identified with the 49ers' "Team of the '80s," got much of the family's stock and real estate holdings in the deal, but remained out of football.

The 49ers struggled through a 6–10 season in 2000 with a young team that featured a rebuilt defense. The revamped unit regularly relied on five rookie starters, among them linebacker Julian Peterson, who blossomed into a Pro Bowl performer.

Garcia also came around as the team's quarterback, throwing for a club record 4,287 yards and earning the first of three straight trips to the Pro Bowl. His ascension, along with that of wide receiver Terrell Owens and the surprising development of the team's young defense, would generate another 49ers' resurgence.

This one didn't have the staying power of the dynastic teams of the past. But it would have its moments, peaking in 2002 when the 49ers won their first NFC West title in five years and headed to the playoffs for the second season in a row.

Unlike the previous season, when the 49ers hit the road as a wild card only to lose narrowly at Green Bay, San Francisco opened its 2002 playoff chase at home against the New York Giants. Not that the home field seemed to make much difference at first, because the Giants, behind the passing of Kerry Collins, stormed to a 38–14 third-quarter lead. But the 49ers resolutely began what would become the NFL's second-largest postseason comeback, stringing together 25 straight points for a 39–38 victory.

It started with Terrell Owens's touchdown catch and subsequent reception for a 2-point conversion, neither of which did much to shake a Giants team brimming with confidence. Indeed, as Owens celebrated in the end zone, offensive coordinator Greg Knapp recalled New York Giants defensive end Michael Strahan going over to the 49ers wide receiver and pointing to the scoreboard. "It was like he was saying, 'That doesn't mean anything. You're still way down. You're still losing,'" Knapp said. "The thing was, we had enough veteran players so that the team didn't panic and say, 'It's over.' We'd been through enough to know that we could fight our way back into it."

Down by 24 points with four minutes left in the third quarter, the 49ers' comeback began with the decision to go to the no-huddle. The quickened pace dovetailed with Jeff Garcia's playmaking on the run, and suddenly the Giants' defense seemed to be on its heels. "I really started to sense then that we could come back, that we could turn this around," Garcia said. "The fact is we were able to put a drive together after we went to the no-huddle. We went down the field and scored those points just before the third quarter ended, so we still had a whole quarter to work with.

"More so than that, I saw their offense starting to shut it down. They weren't as aggressive, and I really felt that played into the hands of our defense. They felt they had a comfortable lead and were trying to work the clock. But I felt they were giving us an opportunity to get back in the game."

In quick succession, Garcia scored on a 14-yard run, completed a second 2-point conversion to Owens, and, after a Jeff Chandler field goal, threw a 13-yard touchdown pass to Tai Streets to complete a string of 25 straight points and put the 49ers on top by 1. At the same time, the 49ers defense, shredded in the game's first three quarters by Giants quarterback Kerry Collins, finally tightened up in the fourth. "We just came together as a group at that point and said, 'They're not going to score again,'" linebacker Jeff Ulbrich recounted. "And they didn't. When Jeff and the offense began moving the ball, we all just started to feel like it was going to happen. In the end, we got the chance to point at the scoreboard."

But only after a wild finish that left 49ers players exhilarated,

*Jeff Garcia celebrates the 49ers' 39–38 playoff victory over the New York Giants on January 5, 2003.*

Paul Sakuma/AP

the crowd at Candlestick Park drained, and the New York Giants beside themselves after they bungled a potential game-winning field goal at the end. "I wish that I could just bottle up that moment—the feeling in the air when that game was over with, the crowd's excitement, and everything that was going on in that stadium," Garcia said. "People basically had been taken on a roller-coaster ride. As a player, you can't afford to go through that up-and-down cycle, but as a fan you can't control anything. You're at the mercy of the players and you're at the mercy of the game. It was just one of those days that now is a piece of history and NFL lore."

The comeback stands out as the second biggest ever in the playoffs and the second biggest in club history. Joe Montana and the 49ers overcame a 28-point deficit in their 38–35 overtime victory over New Orleans in 1980. The greatest deficit overcome in the NFL postseason featured Buffalo beating Houston 41–38 in 1993 after trailing by 32 points.

The good vibes for the 49ers didn't last beyond the second round. Their season crashed to a halt at Tampa Bay, where they were routed by that season's eventual Super Bowl champion. Three days later, in a move that remains stunning despite the long-running friction between Mariucci and the 49ers' brass, which included both the 49ers owner and their general manager, Terry Donahue, the coach was fired. Once again the 49ers were lurching in a different direction. In some ways Mariucci's sudden departure was as surprising as his 1997 entry in place of George Seiffert.

George Seifert had won two Super Bowls. He had the best winning percentage of any coach in NFL history at the time. But after a January 4, 1997, playoff loss at Green Bay in a game played in miserably cold, wet, and muddy conditions, he sounded like a man on the defensive against a demanding organization—his own. "It's unfortunate that we've gotten to be recognized in the league as the team that immediately starts cannibalizing ourselves," Seifert said in the chill of the locker room following the 49ers' 35–14 loss to Green Bay. "Even players were talking about if we lose this game, the bus is driving up to the facility."

Fewer than two weeks later, the 49ers put Seifert on that bus and drove him away. He was replaced by the fresh-faced, exuberant, offensive-minded Steve Mariucci, who made the jump after a year as the head coach at the University of California at Berkeley. Before that he was Brett Favre's quarterbacks coach in Green Bay for four years.

The day Mariucci signed his 49ers' contract, team president Carmen Policy told him, "Steve, you're in for the ride of your life." Mariucci rode the roller coaster for six years, going to the playoffs on four occasions. His stay coincided with some of the team's most tumultuous times—the crumbling of the 49ers' dynasty, severe salary-cap problems, and massive roster turnover. He also endured a running personality clash with his best player, wide receiver Terrell Owens, and weathered uncertainties even as he oversaw the team's resurgence.

But he also had flirted with the idea of taking jobs elsewhere—Notre Dame and Tampa Bay were among the teams showing interest—which irritated owner John York. When York fired him in the days after the 49ers' second-round playoff loss at Tampa Bay in January 2003, York said the dismissal had nothing to do with his job performance and everything to do with so-called "philosophical differences." In dismissing him, York said they couldn't see eye-to-eye on matters big and small. To this day, Mariucci, who became the Detroit Lions coach, says he doesn't know what York is talking about.

Dennis Erickson left Oregon State to replace Mariucci after a month-long coaching search led by general manager Terry Donahue. In two years Erickson won only nine of thirty-two games but was continually hamstrung by a roster stripped down by salary-cap problems and injuries. Donahue said during the spring of 2004 that the 49ers were going to have to take their "medicine" if they were to restore the team's cap health. That proved to be the prelude to a round of cap-driven player releases that resulted in the loss of eight starters, seven on the offense, including Garcia, Owens, Garrison Hearst, Derrick Deese, and Ron Stone.

The results were disastrous, with the team going 2–14. York, who was portrayed as a tightfisted, meddlesome owner, took a public relations beating. The discouragement among fans of the team also was palpable. Toward the end of the season, games at Monster Park were played before a listless crowd. A lot of people in the stands simply left before the game was finished, leaving the 49ers to finish the games in the subdued atmosphere of a near-empty stadium.

In the end, York fired both Erickson and Donahue, eating more than $10 million in their yet-to-be-finished contracts. "Everyone recognizes their dedicated efforts," York said in announcing the dismissals on January 5, 2005. "However, we have decided that a fresh start is in everyone's best interests. We are going to use the extreme disappointment that we all have felt as our turning point. We know how much passion 49ers fans have, and we understand that this is unacceptable to our fans. We need our fans to know that it is equally unacceptable to us." A two-week search followed, and the new coach York hired to

guide the team into the future, Mike Nolan, turned out to have very distinct and sentimental links to the 49ers' past.

Pro Football Hall of Fame linebacker Dave Wilcox easily pictured Mike Nolan as a ten-year-old, running errands in between making mischief at the 49ers' summer training camp. "All we wanted from him was to get us more Gatorade and socks," Wilcox said with a laugh.

Back in 1968 maybe that's all that was expected from the son of 49ers coach Dick Nolan. Well, that and running down balls, collecting other gear, and perhaps helping the team's resident prankster, defensive tackle Charlie Krueger, pull off a practical joke or two on unsuspecting teammates.

His job has gotten considerably more complex since then. The eighteen-year NFL assistant who most recently spent three seasons as the Baltimore Ravens' defensive coordinator returned to the 49ers as their head coach. His January 19, 2005, appointment came thirty-seven years after his father began an eight-season run as the team's head coach. One of the first things the younger Nolan did as the 49ers' new coach was to thank his dad, his first football teacher. "He was the one that taught me that football was a people business and not just an Xs and Os business," Mike Nolan said.

For the younger Nolan, the people part of the business included players such as John Brodie, Gene Washington, Ted Kwalick, Len Rohde, Forrest Blue, Cas Banaszek, Woody Peoples, Krueger, and Wilcox, just to name a few. They were at once his childhood pals and childhood heroes. As his mind raced in the sleepless hours before he took the podium at San Francisco's Mark Hopkins Hotel to formally accept the job, Nolan said it dawned on him that they also were the reason he

# Head Coaches

Mike Nolan took over in 2005 as the fifteenth head coach in 49ers' history. Here's how his predecessors fared (record includes post-season games):

| Years | Coach | Record |
|---|---|---|
| 1950–54 | Lawrence (Buck) Shaw | 33–25–2 |
| 1955 | Norman (Red) Strader | 4–8–0 |
| 1956–58 | Frankie Albert | 19–17–1 |
| 1959–63 | Howard (Red) Hickey | 27–27–1 |
| 1963–67 | Jack Christiansen | 26–38–3 |
| 1968–75 | Dick Nolan | 56–56–5 |
| 1976 | Monte Clark | 8–6–0 |
| 1977 | Ken Meyer | 5–9–0 |
| 1978 | Pete McCulley | 1–8–0 |
| 1978 | Fred O'Connor | 1–6–0 |
| 1979–88 | Bill Walsh | 102–63–1 |
| 1989–96 | George Seifert | 108–35–0 |
| 1997–2002 | Steve Mariucci | 60–43–0 |
| 2003–4 | Dennis Erickson | 9–23–0 |

Note: Hickey resigned after three games in 1963; McCulley was released after nine games in 1978.

played football and later made coaching his life's work. "I know why I love the game, and it was because of those players," said Nolan. "Growing up around those guys and the way that they loved the game and the way they played it."

Nolan's passionate approach to coaching and the depth of his feeling for the 49ers were among the reasons he won over owner John York; Paraag Marathe, the assistant to the general manager; and Terry Tumey, assistant director of football administration. The three ran the search, along with York's son, Jed. The younger York participated with his father in the informal interviews of the five candidates, which occurred over dinner the night before the formal sessions with the panel. "We couldn't be more confident," John York said. "Mike is the perfect choice to lead the 49ers back to the top. We are handing him the San Francisco 49ers, and we expect him to win."

For his part, Nolan embraced the daunting task of reversing the fortunes of a team that wound up a league-worst 2–14 in 2004, matching the club record for losses in a season. His father said his son spent a lifetime preparing for just that kind of challenge. "When he'd work for me at training camp, he'd ask if he could sit in on the team meetings and I told him, 'Come on in,'" the elder Nolan recalled. "He probably picked up a thing or two from that and a lot more along the way. I just think he's always put himself in position to be a coach and a good one. He's got a big job on his hands. But he'll handle it. He'll be fine."

# About the Author

**Dennis Georgatos** followed the 49ers as a youth growing up in the San Francisco Bay Area in the late 1960s and 1970s. He began his career with United Press International in Los Angeles before moving in 1981 to San Diego, where he worked nine years for the Associated Press, spending time covering the San Diego Chargers and San Diego Padres. He has covered the 49ers for the past fourteen years, first for the AP and then with the *San Jose Mercury News*.